T0330659

Reading John Maynard Keynes

This book focuses on understanding the thinking of one of the greatest economists of the 20th century, John Maynard Keynes (JMK), stressing the evolution of his thinking from adherence to the classic Quantity Theory of Money to the development of his own novel theories of unemployment, stagnation and instability in modern capitalism and the need to have active policies to combat these malaises.

The author dissects Keynes's three main analytical works that shaped his thinking and policy recommendations: *A Tract on Monetary Reform* (1923); *A Treatise on Money* (1930); and *The General Theory of Employment, Interest and Money* (1936). This book undertakes a direct analysis of the texts of each of these three books themselves, rather than drawing on secondary literature studying what Keynes "wanted to say" according to other authors sympathetic or unsympathetic with Keynes's ideas. It is an ideal text for a reader who wants to know in clear terms the thought of JMK and the historical context in which it evolved and developed.

This book will be of significant interest to scholars, students and social researchers in various fields who are often surrounded by excessively technically oriented books about Keynes that often omit the history of ideas.

Andrés Solimano holds a PhD in economics from MIT and is the Founder and Chairman of the International Center for Globalization and Development (CIGLOB), Santiago, Chile.

Routledge Focus on Economics and Finance

The fields of economics are constantly expanding and evolving. This growth presents challenges for readers trying to keep up with the latest important insights. Routledge Focus on Economics and Finance presents short books on the latest big topics, linking in with the most cutting-edge economics research.

Individually, each title in the series provides coverage of a key academic topic, whilst collectively the series forms a comprehensive collection across the whole spectrum of economics.

Customer Data Sharing Frameworks
Twelve Lessons for the World
Anton Didenko, Natalia Jevglevskaja and Ross P. Buckley

Crowdfunding European Business
Antonella Francesca Cicchiello

The Chief Financial Officer and Corporate Performance
Finance, Governance and Risk
Elżbieta Bukalska, Anna Wawryszuk-Misztal and Tomasz Sosnowski

Artists Labour Market, Cultural Policy and Creative Economy
A Triangular Model in Poland
Dorota Ilczuk, Anna Karpińska, Emilia Cholewicka

Reading John Maynard Keynes
A Short Introduction
Andrés Solimano

For more information about this series, please visit: www.routledge.com/Routledge-Focus-on-Economics-and-Finance/book-series/RFEF

Reading John Maynard Keynes
A Short Introduction

Andrés Solimano

Routledge
Taylor & Francis Group

LONDON AND NEW YORK

First published 2024
by Routledge
4 Park Square, Milton Park, Abingdon, Oxon OX14 4RN

and by Routledge
605 Third Avenue, New York, NY 10158

Routledge is an imprint of the Taylor & Francis Group, an informa business

© 2024 Andrés Solimano

British Library Cataloguing-in-Publication Data
A catalogue record for this book is available from the British Library

Library of Congress Cataloging-in-Publication Data
Names: Solimano, Andrés, author.
Title: Reading John Maynard Keynes : a short introduction / Andrés Solimano.
Description: Abingdon, Oxon ; New York, NY : Routledge, 2024. | Series: Routledge focus on economics and finance | Includes bibliographical references and index. | Contents: Historical background: the unstable 1920s and the depressive 1930s — A tract on monetary reform. The evil of inflation and the management of money and foreign exchanges — A treatise on money. Wicksell, bulls and bears — The general theory of employment, interest and money. A new macroeconomics of depression — Interpreting Keynes macroeconomics and its relevance for the 21st century.
Identifiers: LCCN 2024008140 (print) | LCCN 2024008141 (ebook) | ISBN 9781032769998 (hardback) | ISBN 9781032770017 (paperback) | ISBN 9781003480785 (ebook)
Subjects: LCSH: Keynes, John Maynard, 1883-1946. | Keynesian economics. | Economics—Philosophy.
Classification: LCC HB103.K47 S65 2024 (print) | LCC HB103.K47 (ebook) | DDC 330.15/6—dc23/eng/20240309
LC record available at https://lccn.loc.gov/2024008140
LC ebook record available at https://lccn.loc.gov/2024008141

ISBN: 978-1-032-76999-8 (hbk)
ISBN: 978-1-032-77001-7 (pbk)
ISBN: 978-1-003-48078-5 (ebk)

DOI: 10.4324/9781003480785

Typeset in Times New Roman
by codeMantra

Contents

Acknowledgements   *vii*

1   Introduction   1

2   Historical Background: The Unstable 1920s and the
    Depressive 1930s   16

3   *A Tract on Monetary Reform.* The Evil of Inflation
    and the Management of Money and Foreign Exchanges   36

4   *A Treatise on Money.* Wicksell, Bulls and Bears   57

5   *The General Theory of Employment, Interest and
    Money*: A New Macroeconomics of Depression   80

6   Interpreting "Keynes Macroeconomics" and Its
    Relevance for the 21st Century   98

    References   *111*
    Index   *117*

Acknowledgements

I would like to acknowledge several people who have contributed in different ways to this work. Thomas G. Good provided very valuable support in editing the manuscript and in untiringly researching and helping to interpret relevant literature for such a vast topic as the macroeconomics of J.M. Keynes. Edgardo Barandiarán, a former professor of mine in the 1970s of monetary theory, provided generous and useful comments and guidance on the structure of this book. Kristina Abbotts, Senior Editor in Economics and Finance at Routledge, was very supportive of the overall project, always keeping a keen eye on its potential readership. Pedro Solimano provided encouragement and motivating reactions by reading an initial draft. Alberto Barrientos Olavarria referred to me other books published on Keynes in recent years. Comments by three anonymous referees are appreciated as they helped to sharpen the content and messages of the book.

1 Introduction

John Maynard Keynes, JMK for short, was an enlightened and innovative academic advisor of several British governments, a successful participant in the stock market and a cosmopolitan and cultured man of public affairs. His interests spanned over a wide variety of subjects including logic and philosophy, economics, probability theory, international affairs, and others. He was an active supporter of art, which was a passion throughout his life. The hyper-specialised economist of today, living in a sort of "ivory tower" largely detached from the real world, is a far cry from the versatility of conceptual backgrounds and interests that made up the personality of John Maynard Keynes more than 100 years ago.

He interacted in various capacities with philosophers like G.E. Moore, Bertrand Russell, Ludwig Wittgenstein and Frank Ramsey; and with main economists such as Alfred Marshall, Edgeworth, Pigou, Hayek, Robbins, Robertson and others. He shared common literary and aesthetic interests with art critics Roger Fry and Clive Bell, writers such as Virginia Wolff, painters Duncan Grant and Vanessa Bell, and more. JMK was a member of the Bloomsbury Group in London interacting with close friends and discussing art, ethics, morals, pacifism, war and other subjects. In the Versailles Conference of 1919, he directly dealt with public leaders such as Lloyd George, Clemenceau, Wilson and Roosevelt and other important political leaders. Few economists had direct contact and influence with such a distinguished array of characters in their lifetime as JMK.

Keynes lived in the complex and turbulent world of the first half of the 20th century that comprised two, very deadly, world wars; the onset of a socialist regime in Russia; the rise and defeat of fascism in Italy and Nazism in Germany; persecutions; hatred; and violence along with, on the positive side, the development of new thinking and culture and technological breakthroughs such as the expansion of telecommunications, mass production of textiles, automobiles, housing for the consumer market and so on.

Keynes witnessed the suspension of the gold standard in the 1910s, the attempt of reconstructing it in the mid-1920s and its abandonment, sequentially in different countries, between 1931 and 1936 in years of economic depression.

DOI: 10.4324/9781003480785-1

The first half of the 1920s was a period of hyperinflation in Germany, Poland, Austria, Hungary and Russia. In Britain, from 1922 to 1936, there was economic stagnation and high unemployment. The United States suffered a stock market crash in 1929 that marked an abrupt end to the "roaring 1920s". That big financial shock preceded the great depression of the first half of the 1930s in America, Europe and the periphery of the world economy.

The second half of the 1930s saw a process of rearmament in Germany and Japan as preparation for a new war. In the 1940s, a new deadly war took place, and Europe had to reconstruct itself and the international monetary system after WWII.

JMK served as an advisor to the British Treasury in the 1910s in the India Office in London. In the Treasury, he provided advice on how to finance World War I, and in 1919, he was part of the official British delegation to Versailles, but then in Paris, he decided to resign from the position for his disagreement with the punitive reparations imposed on Germany, which he correctly anticipated could not be paid without producing severe economic and social dislocations with the economic resources available to defeated Germany.

JMK warned that onerous war reparations would produce undue hardship to the German people opening the road to social destabilisation and political polarisation in the Weimar Republic, a process that soon spilled over with tensions transmitted to the rest of Europe. He was convinced that economic strain reflected in inflation, unemployment, stagnation, and monetary and fiscal disorders can lead to political fragility and eventually to political extremism and authoritarianism including the road to war. In short, he was a strong believer that a dysfunctional economy was inimical for preserving a stable democracy.

In the early 1940s, Keynes served again in the UK's Treasury as adviser to the Chancellor of the Exchequer formulating plans to finance the ongoing international conflict of the first half of the 1940s. His pamphlet *How to Pay for the War* developed policies aimed to mobilise resources for the war without producing undue inflation was an early blueprint on how to devise sensible economic planning. He also served as an advisor in the boards of important private insurance companies; he was a bursar at King's College and played successfully in the stock market on his own behalf and for Cambridge University generating big financial wealth for the affiliated institutions and for himself. In addition, capitalising on the selling success of *The Economic Consequences of the Peace* and his growing reputation as a very clever economist, he was in high demand for writing (earning handsomely) for various newspapers. In fact, he was a European correspondent for *The Manchester Guardian* in the Genoa Convention of 1922 and commented for many years on world economic affairs and British events for *The Nation and Atheneum, The Nation, The New Statesman* and other newspapers.

A direct involvement in unstable financial markets was very helpful, besides profitable, to Keynes in the formulation of theories of bearish and bullish financial investment, the theory of the demand for money, the analysis of investment and appreciation of the speculative features of the stock market in a capitalist economy driven by profits and herd behaviour. His understanding of the role played by the state of expectations and opinion of the business community, always very sensitive to politics and the stance of public policies, related to his practical involvement with the world of capitalist finance. It is evident that Keynes' economic theories were not developed in the isolated campuses of academia although he served, during his whole adult age, as an academic fellow – a don using the English term – at Kings College in Cambridge University.

The outstanding talent of JMK allowed him to blend, in imaginative and creative ways, economic theory and public policy informed by political judgments, philosophy, economics and a familiarity with the international scenario. Keynes was a man of several economic plans produced at the right time when they were required. In addition, he was a practical person besides being an enlightened intellectual. He never had a ministerial position in the British government but was the leading figure of the Committee on Finance and Industry (the Macmillan Committee, 1929–1931) and of the Economic Advisory Council (1930–1939) among other positions. He thought that to be effective in the real world, reality must be understood in its own terms and cannot be forced to fit unsuitable theories developed for other contexts.

Literature on Keynes

There is already a vast bibliography on Keynes. Contributions of the last 50–60 years are selectively cited here. The Royal Economic Society in the early 1970s organised the publication of all Keynes' writings including his articles, books, pamphlets, and personal and professional correspondence under the heading *The Collected Writings of John Maynard Keynes*, comprising 30 volumes edited over several years by Austin Robinson and Donald Moggridge. Volume I corresponds to the first book of Keynes: *Indian Currency and Finance* (Keynes, 2013 [1913]), and other volumes include the books analysed in this book: *A Tract on Monetary Reform* (Keynes, 2000 [1923]) ; *A Treatise on Money* (Keynes, 2011 [1930]); and *The General Theory of Employment, Interest and Money* (Keynes, 1964 [1936]).

Main biographies of JMK are *The Life of John Maynard Keynes* written by Roy Harrod (Harrod, 1951) followed decades later by Moggridge's *Maynard Keynes: An Economist's Biography* (Moggridge, 1992) and Skidelsky's *John Maynard Keynes* in Three Volumes: Vol. I, *Hopes Betrayed*; Vol. II, *The Economist as Savior*; and Vol. III: *Fighting for Freedom, 1937–1946* (Skidelsky, 1992, 2000). In *The Essential Keynes* (Skidelsky, 2015), the author provides a commented exposition of excerpts of JMK's main writings. Another very readable book is *Keynes: The Twentieth Century's Most Influential Economist* (Clarke, 2009). Both books were written in the aftermath of the financial crisis of 2008–2009 which brought a renewed interest in Keynes that had faded away since the so called "crisis of Keynesian economics" in the 1970s.

Among the books analysing Keynes' monetary theory and macroeconomics, we can include *The Years of High Theory* (Shackle, 1967), *On Keynesian Economics and the Economics of Keynes: A Study in Monetary Theory* (Leijonhufvud, 1968), *John Maynard Keynes* (Minsky's 1975 [2008]), *Keynes' Monetary Thought: A Study of Its Development* (Patinkin, 1976), *Maynard's Revenge* (Taylor, 2010) and *Raising Keynes: A Macroeconomics for the 21ˢᵗ Century* (Marglin, 2021). Work in a political economy vein includes *Keynes Against Capitalism: His Economic Case for Liberal Socialism* (Crotty, 2019) among others. Recent books on JMK, oriented to a broader public, include *The Price of Peace: Money, Democracy, and the Life of John Maynard Keynes* (Carter, 2020) and *The Economics of John Maynard Keynes* (Terra, 2023).

Keynes' Talents and Interests

Keynes, using his broad knowledge, clarity of thinking and articulated rhetoric, shaped important debates on a wide number of themes: probability theory, currency, taxation, the stabilisation of money, exchanges and prices, war reparations, the gold standard, the reduction of unemployment, the resumption of growth after a slump, social philosophy and economic inequality, support for the arts, international monetary cooperation and other topics. Given his good reputation in America, he was instrumental in helping to put together the financial loans – lend and lease – from the United States to Britain to finance World War II and help the Soviet Union, France and China. Moreover, he wielded great influence in the set-up of the international monetary system of Bretton Woods and attended, a year before his death and already in a state of fragile health, the inauguration ceremony of the World Bank and the International Monetary Fund.

Keynes was a prolific writer, commanding an elegant writing style, often expressed in common sense language. He was a kind of realist and idealist at the same time, combining a highly logical mentality with a sense of practicality and realism in his proposals. He had ambivalent positions towards capitalism, admiring its potential capacity to mobilise economic resources and apply new technologies but at the same time as a system prone to recession, unemployment and the concentration of wealth in small economic elites. He distinguished between the entrepreneur who creates productive wealth and the rentier who lives out of the incomes accruing from accumulated (and/or inherited) wealth. JMK was critical of greed and "the love of money" as motivators of human behaviour. He wrote on important policy issues for England, his own country; Europe; and the world.

His first book was *Indian Currency and Finance* published in 1913 where he shows how the monetary system of India, then a British colony, worked at the time of the gold standard and the silver standard, the role of the rupee and its interactions with the financial and exchange rate system of the metropolis, England. At the time, India did not have its own central bank.

JMK international influence was greatly boosted by the lucid prediction of his book *The Economic Consequences of Peace* – written in the summer of 1919 and published at the end of that year after resigning to the British delegation to the Treaty of Versailles, in the aftermath of World War I (WWI). As said, Keynes anticipated that the harsh reparations imposed on Germany by the victor nations would lead to economic hardship and could destabilise the fragile German democracy that had emerged from the war. In fact, the birth of the Weimar Republic was not easy, and it was surrounded by social upheavals. His perceptions were tragically prescient as in the 1920s and 1930s a defeated Germany suffered from very high inflation, external debt problems, reparation payments and an erratic capacity to sustain economic progress and job creation. Expectations were often disappointed, and resentment spread through German society leading to a surge of destructive nationalism and extremism at home and, in the 1930s, rearmament and the launching of external expansionism, behind the quest for "Arian supremacy". The result was World War II along with atrocities such as the holocaust and the extermination of the Jews.

The publication of *The Economic Consequences of the Peace* catapulted Keynes to the status of an international star in economics. He was regularly consulted by governments, corporations, the press, and universities on matters of monetary policy, exchange rate, investment policy, international economic relations, and other topics. His prediction and cogent analysis of the feasibility and consequences of the reparations payments imposed on defeated Germany by the Allies made him an early influencer in economic policy thinking in the 1920s.

His study on the theory of probability – *The Treatise on Probability* published in 1921 (14 years after its initiation) – led him to an understanding of the important issue of uncertainty. He showed that in uncertain and volatile contexts, quantitative probabilities of events can be of little use. Keynes argued that people tend to make decisions and find reasonable comfort in uncertain conditions either by extrapolating the past to the future using frequencies of past events or by following the average opinions of their fellow citizens, whether right or wrong. He was against the frequency approach of probability as a guide to the future and favoured an expectational approach in which the role of judgement and the judicious use of new information by the individual and social groups can update prior beliefs. He was also aware of the risks of misperception and the role of waves of enthusiasm and pessimism involved in forming personal expectations according to what others think about certain events and prospects.

Keynes drew at least three main conclusions from his analysis of uncertainty for economic policy design, investment behaviour and financial decisions. Firstly, people were rarely faced with optimal options in uncertain contexts and had to choose, many times, among sub-optimal choices and make a ranking of less preferred situations.

Secondly, inaction in the face of uncertainty is not a good choice as it precludes obtaining potential gains from acting for fear of making mistakes.

Thirdly, planning for the long run, although sensible as an attitude, is subject to more uncertainty the more distant is the planning horizon. He coined the famous phrase "in the long run we are all dead" calling for setting policy objectives for the closer future.

An area of application of these principles is investment analysis, articulated more fully in *The General Theory of Employment, Interest and Money.* He envisaged the entrepreneur as somebody with an inherent tendency to take more risks than the common citizen, in particular the rentier, who prefers earning incomes in a passive way through the acquisition of an interest-yielding asset. In contrast, the entrepreneur is somebody who engages in the actual production of goods and services by hiring workers and putting in place, for that purpose, machines, equipment and structures. He valued and respected those in "industry".

In addition, JMK invested a lot of time in understanding the role of money and liquidity as a hedge to uncertainty. Both *A Treaty on Money* with his analysis of bearish and bullish behaviour in financial markets and *The General Theory* with the theory of liquidity preference elaborate on this important topic.

Keynes wrote on both theory and policy intended for wider audiences and policymakers and not only professional and academic economists. The more policy-oriented articles are put together as *Essays in Persuasion* in *The Collected Writings of John Maynard Keynes*, Vol. IX. A list of topics explored in that volume includes the following:

- Economic reconstruction in Europe after WWI
- War reparations
- The consolidation of war debts mainly to the United States
- The need for loans to Soviet Russia
- Inflation
- The stabilisation of the French franc
- The return and the end of the gold standard
- The calculations of exchange parities and currency misalignments
- Economic slumps
- The banking system in depression
- Political philosophy, laissez faire
- Liberalism and socialism
- How to pay for the war
- The means to prosperity and other topics

He also wrote on a variety of "non-economic" themes. Several pieces can be found in *The Collected Writings of John Maynard Keynes*, Vol. XXVIII: *Social, Political, and Literary Writings* that deal, among others, with the following subjects:

- Morals and ethics
- Political philosophy

- Conservatism, liberalism, socialism and communism
- Marx, D. Hume, Freud, A. Einstein, George Bernard Shaw, H.G. Wells, H. Ibsen and others
- The history of ancient currencies
- The arts include painting, ballet, opera and their public support. In the early 1940s, JMK was appointed as the chairman of the Arts Council of Great Britain in 1931, an institution that he helped to create.

Gambling, bets, lotteries, and documenting payoffs and losses related to these activities are also included. Part of this work was done for the Royal Commission on Lotteries and Betting oriented to pass recommendations about the scope, desirability and scale of gambling activities in the context of proposals for a possible tax on gambling. The commission also reviewed state lotteries. In general, JMK was favourable of gambling subject to certain boundaries; he held the liberal stance of allowing people to indulge themselves in these activities while taking care of exposing participants to financial ruin, fraud and forms of deviant behaviour. He also quantified the revenue potential for the public treasury of state lotteries based on actual records of gambling in the United Kingdom.

The Evolving Macroeconomics of Keynes

This book analyses, mainly, the *macroeconomics of JMK*, including its evolution reflecting the main shift from a focus on the price level to a focus on the level of employment and real income through a new theory.

JMK's main unit of analysis is the whole economy – the macroeconomy – rather than individual markets, individual agents or specific industries. Keynes calls attention that while supply and demand are used as a framework of analysis to determine relative prices and quantities in particular markets, there is no such analysis for the demand and supply for variables such as real national income, total employment and the level of prices. Until the *General Theory,* the common practice in economics was to use Walras' general equilibrium analysis or Marshallian price theory to determine relative prices with the price level being determined "from the outside" say by the Quantity Theory of Money. Keynes, Wicksell and Myrdal were among those who noted this unfitting marriage between the (marginal utility) value theory and the Quantity Theory of Money (see Myrdal 1939 [1965]). Keynes' theory of effective demand exposed in the *General Theory* and its various components tries to escape from this received heritage.

On the contrary, Michal Kalecki, who independently derived a macro theory like Keynes' *General Theory*, did not face the problem of reconciling marginal utility, neo- classical, value theory with macroeconomics as he was (self)formed mainly in the economics of Marx, Tugan-Baranovsky and Rosa Luxembourg.

In addition, JMK warned that trying to extrapolate individual behaviour to aggregate (macro) behaviour can lead to "fallacies of composition". The most well-known example of such fallacy is the "paradox of thrift" in which the attempt to increase saving by the community may lead to a *decline* in aggregate savings if it cuts aggregate consumption, effective demand since savings is a function of income. The more general point is that individual logics are not always consistent with collective outcomes.[1] Macro analysis cannot be reduced to a mechanical extrapolation of micro behaviour.

This book discusses these issues around an analysis of Keynes' three main academic books:

1 *A Tract on Monetary Reform* (TMR)
2 *A Treatise on Money* (TM)
3 *The General Theory of Employment, Interest and Money* (GT)

There is a popular belief that "the macroeconomics of Keynes" is really the macroeconomics of the *General Theory*. However, this is not entirely correct although a large part of his enormous academic and policy influence stems from the analysis of the GT. This book underscores that JMK's work must be examined in a proper historical evolution of his thinking that also includes the *Tract* and the *Treatise*. The core evolution was departing from the quantity theory of money (macro theory) and classic economics (value and distribution theory) in the GT compared with its relative attachment – not wholeheartedly – in the two previous books to these two strands of thought. However, there is no denial of their usefulness: the *Tract* has been very influential over the years for the study of both moderate and extreme inflation, to understand departures of exchange rates from the predictions of the Purchasing Power Parity doctrine and the general management of monetary policy in economies outside the gold standard. In turn, the *Treatise* is extremely rich in its thorough review of alternative forms of money, price indices according to different formulations of the quantity theory of money, the derivation of cost-push and excess demand (investment/savings imbalances) in price formation and the institutional detail of the working of the banking system and its interaction with central banking. In contrast, perhaps surprisingly, institutional detail of the monetary and credit sector is not present in the *General Theory*. In addition, the specification between "financial circulation" and "industrial circulation" and the patterns of "bullish" and "bearish" investor's sentiments precede the theory of the preference for liquidity in the GT and the transaction and speculative motives in the demand for money.

Methodologically and conceptually, it is apparent that there was a tension between JMK's formation in classic economics at Cambridge University and his desire to find new explanations for a variety of economic problems facing capitalism in the first half of the 20th century. In fact, during Keynes' times, capitalism was particularly prone to experience frequent economic crises and maladjustment resulting in inflation (sometimes extreme), currency misalignments, unemployment, banking fragility and depression. To understand these phenomena, JMK wanted to "escape from the traditional ways of thinking" that were too complacent with a do-nothing view of economic stabilisation based on the belief that the free market would solve these problems by itself (policy interventions would only make things worse).

Box 1.1   Marshall, Edgeworth and Pigou

JMK received his theoretical fundamentals in classical economics at King's College, Cambridge University, under the tutelage of Alfred Marshall, Francis Edgeworth and Arthur Cecil Pigou:

Alfred Marshall (1842–1924) – One of the founders of the School of English Neoclassical Economics. He was a professor of political economy at Cambridge. His *Principles of Economics* (1890) was a standard university textbook – introducing the concept of the output of goods as determined by its supply and demand, thus also determining the price of goods. He also distinguished between short-run and long-run equilibrium with prices adjusting in the short run and investment and output in the long run. Major contributions revolved around consumer and producer surplus, substitution and complementarity between goods and price elasticity.

Francis Y. Edgeworth (1845–1926) – He was a professor of political economy at King's College and one of the pioneers of the application of mathematics to the study of economics and statistics (see Edgeworth's *Mathematical Physics*). His contributions revolve around the pure theory of exchange among traders based on indifference curves and marginal utility, exploring the effect of the number of traders on contracting and the nature of equilibrium (core). The "Edgeworth box" shows how an exchange equilibrium is achieved and helped to develop general equilibrium theory in the late 19th century and the 20th century (see Humphrey, 1996).

Arthur Cecil Pigou (1877–1959) – He was an architect of the School of Economics, Cambridge, and a professor of political economy at Cambridge (replacing Professor Marshall). He wrote the *Economics of Welfare* (1920), examining the social benefits of the interplay among the buying, selling and working decisions of individuals and the production and employment decisions of companies. He contributed to economics in several areas such as the functioning of the labour market, the nature of unemployment (mainly frictional and voluntary), externalities, taxation on land and other topics. Keynes maintained good relations with Pigou although he disagreed with his interpretations of unemployment.

In *The General Theory*, Keynes *abandons* key premises of prevailing analysis such as Say's law (supply creates its own demand), full price and wage flexibility, interest rate determination by savings and investment, and automatic full employment; these underlying assumptions were present in the work of Edgeworth, Marshall and Pigou. By abandoning these premises, Keynes would introduce a whole new way of thinking in macroeconomic analysis. This was the main accomplishment of *The General Theory,* which became a theory of income and employment determination in a field previously dominated by a focus on the price level as the main policy concern.

Another common misconception is that Keynes was only an "economist of depression". However, it is apparent that he also was an "economist of inflation", a main theme in the *Tract on Monetary Reform* and the *Treatise on Money.* These two books were devoted to understanding the causes and consequences of the "variations in the value of money".

The shift of JMK towards a new macroeconomics was evolutive. In the *Tract,* he was still attached to the Quantity Theory of Money (QTM), which states that MV = PY where M is the stock of money, V is the velocity of circulation, P is the price level and Y is the real output. This relation is a cornerstone of classic analysis in the study of the price level and inflation (a change in the level of prices). However, JMK distanced himself from the orthodox interpretation of the QTM in which the causality goes from the supply of money to the price level and stressed an *independent* role of the demand for money (the inverse of velocity) in the determination of output and prices. In the *Tract,* he also stressed the behaviour of commercial banks in creating credit and the effects of the central bank in the creation of base money affecting the overall liquidity of the economy.

The emphasis is both behavioural and institutional. His practical suggestions on how to conduct monetary policy and exchange policy for economies that, since WWI, had abandoned the gold standard were novel and became very influential. His proposal calls for an *accommodative monetary policy* to avoid either an excess demand or an excess supply of money to stabilise the price level and smooth out the business cycle. Key instruments for these purposes are the management of the discount rate by the central bank (in his example, the Bank of England, BoE) along with open market operations and the BoE influence on the liquidity ratio of commercial banks. The *Tract* also delves into the distributive impacts of inflation (and deflation) on debtors, creditors, capitalists and workers and identifies the negative effect of high inflation on investment and economic growth. He wrote the *Tract* observing the dynamics of explosive inflation in Germany, Austria and Russia in the early 1920s and elaborated on the concept of the *inflation tax* and the connection between the financing of fiscal deficits with unbacked loans from the central bank to the national treasury with the consequence of inflation. *A Tract* also examines exchange rate determination under the doctrine of Purchasing Power Parity (PPP) associated with the Swedish economist Gustav Cassel and before with David Ricardo. Again, he explores the causes and consequences of deviation of current exchange rates from price level ratios among nations as dictated by the PPP doctrine.

A Treatise on Money, in turn, is a two-volume book written over a six-year period starting in 1924 in a period of stagnation for Great Britain, although his main aim was mainly theoretical, seeking to clarify monetary theory and explain fluctuations in the value of money. The book reviews different types

Textbook 1.2 Main Analytical Features of *A Treatise on Money*

We can highlight the following five main elements that compose the analytical framework of the *Treatise*:

1 A dual price theory cost is based on a distinction between prices of consumption goods, prices of investment goods and an overall price level.
2 The consumer goods price and overall price level formulations are obtained from expenditure-income-based identities. Prices depend on the cost of production such as wages and payments of intermediate inputs ("incomes inflation") and the excess of investment over savings showing up as over-normal (windfall) profits ("commodity inflation" or "profit inflation").
3 The quantity theory of money (QTM) enters as a determinant of the price level in *long-run equilibrium*. The fundamental equations of Keynes and the QTM formulations only coincide when: (a) investment = savings and (b) market interest rate = natural interest rates.
4 The interest rate is determined by the interplay between the supply of savings and the demand for investment, and credit/money creation.
5 The *Treatise* follows the theories of Knut Wicksell (Stockholm School) of the loanable funds market. The TM adopts the distinction between the market interest rate and the natural interest rate that equilibrates savings and investment at full employment. Both rates will coincide in full macro equilibrium, termed as "monetary equilibrium" by Wicksell.
6 *A Treatise* provides a compelling story of *speculative finance* tied to bullish and bearish sentiments in the securities market, financed by savings deposits in the banking system. This process is labelled "financial circulation" referring to the circuit of money devoted to the buying and selling of financial assets/securities as opposed to a circuit of "industrial circulation" in which deposits finance current transactions by individuals (consumption) and payments made by enterprises in productive activities such as hiring labour, buying inputs and so on.

of money (state money, private money) and their functions; it considers issues of price indices and develops a new theory of the price level – the "fundamental equations" – based on income and expenditure identities rather than the quantity equation linking the supply and demand for money with the price level. Methodologically, the book followed a theory of business cycle with sequences of booms and recession rather than an equilibrium theory (static) of the determination of income and employment.

The road from the *Tract* and the *Treatise* to the *General Theory* involved shifting the focus from inflation – relevant for the unstable 1920s – to a theory of income and employment determination suitable for the depressive 1930s. In addition, JMK wanted to develop a completely new view of how macroeconomic systems work in the real world.

The big rupture of the GT with classical economics was in abandoning critical assumptions such as the Say's law (supply creates its own demand), the Quantity Theory of Money (money determines the price level) and interest rate determination by saving and investment (the Wicksellian mechanism). A list of critical departures from the classical analysis undertaken in the GT is given as follows:

i According to the Say's law, an over-supply of goods and over-supply of labour is a logical impossibility if the price system works properly and clears all markets. Keynes – different from today's "New Keynesian" concerned with price rigidities and frictions – rather than focusing on why the price system could fail to do its job decided to replace the supply driven Say's law with the *principle of effective demand* (with total demand equals consumption plus investment in a closed economy). This created a special role for both consumption spending and the demand for investment goods as critical determinants of aggregate employment (rather than the real wage; see Chapters 2 and 3 of the GT).

ii Another theory that the GT forsakes is the determination of the interest rate in the loanable funds market (savings and investment process) and its replacement by its determination in the money market. Moreover, he distinguished between the "market interest rate" (observed in the credit market) and the "natural" interest rate (the rate that equals savings and investment at full employment, a generally unobservable variable). In the *General Theory* that distinction between natural and market interest rate is abandonned. The liquidity preference function (demand for money) is formulated around three main motives: transaction, precaution and speculation.

iii In this context, the interest rate represents the opportunity cost of holding money and must be balanced with the various benefits (conveniences) of holding money such as "being liquid", say the ability to use money for purchases of goods and services immediately. The classic notion of the interest rate as the price of current consumption in terms of future consumption is examined in Chapter 14 of the *General Theory* but Keynes leans in favour of the interest rate as the price of liquidity.

iv Keynes observed that in response to news and shocks, interest rates adjusted, instantaneously, to ensure *stock equilibrium* in asset markets in the short run. The stocks of existing securities were much larger than the flows of new securities offered in the market in a short period of time. The story of interest rate determination by the flows of savings and investment was viewed by JMK as inconsistent with fast-speed adjustment of asset prices and interest rates in response to news and changes in expectations.

v In the GT, a fundamental role is attached to variations in income and employment as the two main adjustment variables in macroeconomic equilibrium when there is an (ex-ante) imbalance between savings and investment. Again, Keynes makes the bold move of replacing the adjustment in the price level with variations in income and employment as the central adjustment variable in the face of discrepancies between planned investment and desired savings. Savings and investment imbalances were introduced in the *Treatise* through the price equation but in the *General Theory* savings and investment disequilibrium drive income and employment changes.

vi It is in the *General Theory* that JMK makes a more systematic application of the consequences of the uncertainty principle on economic outcomes chiefly through the demand for investment and the demand for money. Moreover, uncertainty affects expected income that determines consumption and effective demand.

vii Standard economic theory assumes rational behaviour guided by comparing expected costs and benefits of different decisions. However, if due to uncertainty these expectations are too fragile and unreliable, the stock market – that supposedly governs intertemporal resource allocation – becomes a largely dysfunctional guide to investment decisions. JMK even makes the analogy between investing in the stock market and playing in a casino. This failure of private capital markets underpins JMK calls, in the GT, for the "socialisation of investment" (the state should play a dominant role in the process of capital formation).

viii The focus on explaining business cycles, say sequences of booms and recessions of pre-GT theory (including the *Treatise*), is replaced in the GT by a focus on a stable equilibrium with unemployment and underutilisation of economic resources. This equilibrium tends to be not only a possibility but also a most likely general state of a capitalist economy experiencing chronic lack of effective demand.

ix Fiscal policy, and to a lesser extent monetary policy, must be used actively to stabilise the economy in a situation of slump and collapse of the marginal efficiency of capital due to pessimistic expectations. Keynes argued that an automatic adjustment through price and wage deflation is very unlikely to restore full employment. For JMK, it is a risky and so-cially costly strategy to rely on market forces to restore full employment when an economic system is hit by large shocks that go beyond a fall in demand in a localised market. The distinctive macroeconomic nature of Keynes' analysis must be noted in this connection.

The break with the classic tradition taking place with the publication of *The General Theory of Employment, Interest and Money* (GT) in 1936 created a truly "scientific revolution" accompanied by far-reaching policy implications. The concepts of the principle of effective demand, the marginal propensity to consume, the inducement to invest, the preference for liquidity, the multiplier introduced fresh air to a field dominated by the quantity theory of money and automatic full employment. Keynes shows in *The General Theory* that an equilibrium with unemployment and output below full capacity does exist and can be stable. This was a logical impossibility before; however, the great depression with massive unemployment and bankruptcies of banks and firms shows that it was a very relevant possibility. Keynes demonstrated theoreti-cally the plausibility of an economy with stagnation and unemployment and his vision fitted well with an objective reality of economic depression.

JMK believed that economic systems tended to converge to an equilibrium, but that equilibrium could be sub-optimal and inefficient in the sense that valuable resources remain idle, while at the same time, we live in a world of unsatisfied wants and poverty. Worse, the capitalist system tends to stabilise at such a bad equilibrium that keeps valuable economic resources underutilised. Monetary and fiscal policy could help to overcome an under-employment equilibrium, argued Keynes.

JMK was sceptic that monetary policy alone could be effective to over-come a slump if the interest rate is very low, and the demand for money infi-nitely elastic as the extra money injected to the economy would be absorbed almost entirely by the public as additional monetary balances with no effect on the interest rate and the cost of investment. In addition, if the marginal efficiency of capital, MEC, collapses, the revival of investment requires that "animal spirits" wake up again and pull investment. A simple change in the interest rates that do not turn around expectations and restore optimism in the business community will not do the trick of reviving private investment. The capitalist economy is left depending upon flimsy and uncertain expecta-tions for ensuring an adequate level of capital formation and output growth.

In the conditions of a profound slump that has shattered expectations and created a negative assessment of the future state of the economy, it is better to put in place a programme of public investment of the type that JMK (with Henderson) proposed for England in the pamphlet "Can Lloyd George, do it?" supporting the candidate of the Liberal Party in the general elections of 1929. In this case, a programme of public investment, the injection of purchasing power in the economy is direct – monetary policy acts indirectly – and the effect on effective demand is amplified further by the operation of the multi-plier whose magnitude depends on the marginal propensity to consume. This is the main rationale for using fiscal policy as explained in the *General Theory*.

Organisation of the Book

This book is organised around six chapters including this Introduction (Chapter 1). Chapter 2 provides the historical background against which Keynes' work developed. Chapter 3 offers an analysis of *A Tract on Monetary Reform*, Chapter 4 examines the book *A Treatise on Money*, Chapter 5 studies *The General Theory of Employment, Interest and Money* and Chapter 6 provides a comparative analysis of the three books noting differences and similarities between them, underscoring Keynes relevance for the 21st century.

Note

1 In the field of collective choice, the Arrow's impossibility theorem shows that an aggregate welfare function may not be fully consistent with individual preferences and basic reasonable axioms, see Solimano (2022).

2 Historical Background

The Unstable 1920s and the Depressive 1930s[1]

Introduction

The crisis of the globalised market order prevailing in the period 1870–1914 had profound consequences for the first half of the 20th century. The first wave of globalisation (c.1870–1913) was a period of open trade regimes, financial integration and significant flows of migration between the "old world" (Europe) and the "new world" (North America, Argentina, Australia, Brazil and a score of other countries located in the periphery of the world economy). This was a period of low-trade tariffs and few restrictions to the mobility of capital. International migration was freer but not completely (individuals from Chinese origin and other people from the Far East faced serious problems to settle in countries such as Australia and the United States).[2]

Britain was a main industrial centre and a net capital exporter to the rest of the world, reflecting its structural excess savings relative to home investment. The dominant role played by Britain in the first wave of globalisation was underpinned by its large influence on the global trade system, supply of loanable funds and foreign direct investment. This, in turn, was helped by two important factors: her naval superiority and the role played by the Bank of England in steering the gold standard.

However, this dominance started to be challenged by rising powers such as the recently unified nations of Germany and Italy besides France. The Russian, Ottoman, Habsburg and Japanese empires also had a role in the division of the world into colonies, protectorates and areas of influence. Another potential challenger was the United States endowed by a vast territory, an enterprising population, new technologies and natural resources.

The main economies of the capitalist core were developing rapidly, supported by the introduction of railways, steamship, telecommunication systems and other technical innovations applied to production, distribution and trade. Keynes was marvelled by the conveniences and comfort that the pre-1914 economic order brought about but at the same time was conscious of the fragility and vulnerability of that order (see his introductory chapter to *The Economic Consequences of the Peace*, Keynes, 1971 [1920]).

DOI: 10.4324/9781003480785-2

The system was supported by a system of balance of power among various dynasties such as the British monarchy, the Kaiser in Germany, the Tzar family in Russia, the Austro-Hungarian monarchy and the Ottoman monarchy. It was a world of empires, cooperation and competition for the conquest of the world and for taking advantage of the benefits of economic integration.

Karl Polanyi in *The Great Transformation* published in the 1940s (Polanyi, 1944) stated that the civilisation of the 19th century rested on four main institutions: (i) a balance of power among nations, (ii) the gold standard, (iii) the unregulated market economy and (iv) the liberal state. The arrangements/institutions (i) and (ii) were national and the (iii) and (iv), were national. Likewise (i) and (iv) were political and (ii) and (iii) economical.

This world of material prosperity and apparent stability, however, had its own internal contradictions: income and wealth were unequally distributed and conflicts between working classes and economic elites developed. The fruits of globalisation were shared unevenly between labour and capital, generating significant levels of inequality.[3]

The European revolutions of 1848 and the Paris Commune in 1872 showed that social conflict accompanied the dynamic but disruptive capitalist system that created new goods and novel technologies but along the way also generated social dislocation. Employment in the factory system was often characterised by long hours, the use of child work and few labour rights.

In the last quarter of the 19th century and early 20th century, there was also a process of economic concentration in ownership and market shares in the productive and financial spheres with the formation of monopolies and oligopolies in a style of "monopoly capitalism".

World War I (WWI)

World War I interrupted abruptly the first wave of globalisation and entailed the death of nearly 12 million people and the massive destruction of physical infrastructure and valuable economic assets.[4] Moreover, it disrupted economic globalisation and led to the abandoning of the gold standard, two cornerstones of the global economic order prevailing until 1913. At the same time, the war had expansionary effects on the economies of the United States that joined the conflict just in 1917 and Britain but it exerted devastating effects on Austro-Hungarian empire and the Russian empire that could not withstand the combined effect of the reorientation of their economies towards the defence sector, the economic and social burden of fighting in the war and the existence of food scarcities. The two empires were administratively weak, and the war exacerbated this feature. In addition, the war devastated the German economy, and the French economy also suffered.

As of 1913, the world became divided into three camps that evolved as the war developed: (i) the *Allied Powers* comprising, in the first phase (1914/1915), the countries of the triple entente, France, the United Kingdom and Russia, to which were joined in a second phase (1915/1916) by Italy, Portugal and Romania. In a third phase (1917/1918), Russia dropped out but the United States joined in along with Brazil, Greece, Siam and China; (ii) the *Central Powers,* at the start of the war in 1914, included Germany, the Austro-Hungarian empire and the Ottoman Empire. They were joined also by Bulgaria in 1915; and (iii) *neutral nations* such as Sweden and Switzerland.

Textbox 2.1 The Rise and Fall in Military Spending

The increase in military spending following the outbreak of WWI was sharp. In the United Kingdom, military outlays increased from about 4 percent of GDP in 1913 to 38 percent in 1916–1917. After the war, military spending declined to 4 percent of GDP in 1920 after having reached 32 percent in 1918. Military expenditure in the United States went up from 1 percent of GDP in 1914–1916 to 6 percent in 1917 and 13 percent in 1918.[5] The rise in military spending probably stimulated *aggregate* economic activity in Britain and the United States.

Germany engaged in the most ambitious increase in defence spending in WWI with a rise from 4.9 percent of GDP in 1913 to 53 percent in 1917. This implied the redeployment of both labour and capital towards its armament factories, chemical industries, shipyards and other activities linked to the military preparation for the Great War. In contrast with the USA and the UK, the sustained increase in military spending in Germany coincided with a *drop* in output/income whose magnitude varies according to the different estimates (Solimano, 2020).

In Austro-Hungary, defence spending increased from about 4 percent of GDP in 1913 to 30 percent in 1914 and then stabilised at 26 percent in 1916–1917. This swift resource reallocation towards the defence sector was also followed by a *steady decline* in national income from 1914 to 1918 of very large magnitude, resembling closely the contraction in Germany. Of course, as war was fought in the territories of Germany and Austro-Hungary, this should have contributed to the decline in aggregate output in these countries.

The decline in military spending *after* the war probably entertained recessionary impulses.[6] The return to a peaceful economy is not an automatic process and can produce frictional unemployment and supply disruptions. Moreover, the decline in military spending is bound to reduce the demand stimulus to the economy.

To this list, we must also add the colonies, protectorates of the ruling empires that provided raw materials and food to the metropolis to help them in the war effort.

The surge of inflation because of the war was also a problem, and it was a main theme of *A Tract on Monetary Reform*. Inflation was initially repressed; however, when price controls were relaxed, it came in the open. Because of price surges, the real value of liquid savings accumulated during the war declined creating a negative wealth effect. Moreover, private investment took time to recover due to various uncertainties[7] such as the size and timing of war reparations and the new trade relations with newly emerging countries after the breakup of the four empires that ruled before WWI. The social landscape had changed, and labour unions became more active and influential. In turn, the redefinition of territories and tax bases affected the ability of governments to collect taxes and central banks provided loans to the government affecting monetary stability. In addition, the lack of complementary physical infrastructure (roads, ports, telecommunications) damaged by the war also must have hampered the recovery of private investment.

After the war, belligerent countries had accumulated internal and external debts while they had huge needs of resources to provide income and housing support to demobilised war combatants and jump-start the civilian sector. In addition, Germany and the former Austro-Hungarian empire lost territories and were forced to pay war reparations to victor nations. Keynes never recommended increasing military spending or launching wars to stimulate effective demand. His preferred way to increase effective demand was to boost public works for civilian purposes.

Effects on Economic Activity

The effects of World War I on GDP per capita varied substantially across different countries of the Allied Camp and the Central Powers. The per capita GDP of France, Germany, Italy, Austria and Russia was lower in 1918 than in 1913. The magnitudes of the contractions in GDP per head go from 5 percent in Italy to 53 percent in Russia, with France's per capita GDP in 1918 being 31 percent lower than in 1913. In contrast, in 1918, the per capita GDP of Britain was 11 percent higher and nearly 7 percent higher in the USA than in 1913 according to Maddison's data.

The breakout of the war in 1914 caught the US economy in a recession affected by financial instability. Prices in the stock exchange market sharply declined at the beginning of the war as Europeans started a sell-off of US stocks. Also, a run-on commercial bank was developed. Nevertheless, things turned around thereafter led by increased European demand for food and munition that were needed to support the European population and the waging of war. From the viewpoint of America, this created an economic stimulus with beneficial effects on agriculture and the industrial sector.

Broader Consequences of World War I

World War I changed forever the geopolitical landscape of the world. The balance of power that existed until 1913 collapsed, and it could not be restored. The Austro-Hungarian,[8] Russian, Ottoman and Prussian empires ceased to exist and new national borders prompted population movements and new economic relations among nations. The Bolshevik revolution, embracing a direct challenge to the capitalist system and the ensuing loss of the pre-war economic relations with the West would not have been possible without the collapse of the Tzars' empire induced by the economic crisis and social exhaustion stemming from the war.

The United States did not participate in important milestones of the post-war settlement. It was not part of the recently created League of Nations and formally abstained from participating in the Conference of Genoa of 1922 to agree on the contours of the economic and financial foundations of the reconstruction of Europe and the restoration of the gold standard. However, it played an important financing role to recycle war reparations settled in Versailles. Nonetheless, this funding was not enough to avoid destabilisation of the Weimar Republic. Keynes advocated a cancellation of debts between the Allies and a cancellation of debts with Russia. For him, past debts were a drag on economic reconstruction and recovery and the hurdle had to be removed. Nonetheless, the involved parties had a different opinion.

Germany emerged from the conflict bloated by external debts and reparations payments imposed in the Treaty of Versailles and the peace treaties of Saint German and Trianon (the Russians were not invited to the Paris Conference) . The Treatise of Versailles between the Allied Powers and the German Weimar Republic besides imposing economic reparations also led to the end of the German colonies in Africa and the Southern Pacific and the disarmament of Germany. The rise of Adolf Hitler was, probably, the grandchild of injured national pride following the Treaty and the explosive inflation in 1922 and 1923 that destabilised the fragile Weimar Republic. Extreme monetary instability and hyperinflation also affected Austria, Hungary, Poland and Soviet Russia between 1921 and 1923.

The Genoa conference of 1922, attended by Keynes and convened by Lloyd George, was oriented to the reconstruction of the international monetary system along the lines of a "gold exchange standard" resembling the pre-1914 monetary standard. However, the endeavour was problematic as the world had changed substantially with the Great War. Previous exchange rate parities were largely obsolete after the big changes that brought about the war. A return to the parameters of the old economic order was unrealistic, a point reiterated by JMK who was in the 1920s against the return of the exchange parities prevailing in 1913.

Towards the end of the decade, in 1929, a serious stock market crash affected the United States and triggered a global recession. Economics and international politics contributed to turning a financial shock (the stock market crash of October of 1929) into a depression. A list of relevant factors is the following: exchange rates were in part misaligned, commercial banks in Europe and America were exposed to financial fragility, the prevalence of a ruling orthodoxy in which it was very important to keep fiscal budgets balanced, preserving the gold standard and maintaining free trade over objectives of full employment and urgent recovery. Keynes argued against the "Treasury view" and the "Bank of England view" that represented this economic orthodoxy. Politically, he sided with Lloyd George and supported George's position that the priority was to reduce unemployment in Britain and overcome the stagnation of the economy.

The lack of an international hegemon able to take leadership in international coordination in economic matters was another factor that contributed to the great depression of the early 1930s. The UK was a declining empire unable to perform this role, and the USA was an emerging superpower that was still reluctant to take this responsibility.

Textbox 2.2   Social Unrest, Revolutions and Soviet Russia

The end of WWI gave rise to a period of acute social activism in several European countries. There were workers' councils and factory takeovers in Germany in 1918–1919 with uprisings in Berlin and Munich; in Hungary, there was the Aster Revolution in 1918 and the Hungarian Soviet Revolution of 1919; in Italy, there were factory councils in Turin in 1919; and general strikes in Turin and Milan in 1920. In these episodes, workers' democracy challenged the political status quo, and the workers took leading roles in the general management of enterprises as an open challenge to the rule of capital.

In Italy, Antonio Gramsci and Palmiro Togliatti, then editors of the magazine *L'Ordine Nuovo* (later closed by Mussolini), claimed that workers' democracy would emancipate the workforce from the alienation and disaffection process typical of the capitalist factory. Moreover, they thought that workers' democracy was an embryonic development that could lead to revolutionary change and transformation of the state.[9]

In Russia, after the February Revolution in 1917 and learning the lessons of the crushing of the Paris Commune, the Bolsheviks managed to prevail and captured the government.

The workers' committees called Soviets, in alliance with intellectuals, political leaders and military strategists, such as Lenin and Trotsky, took power on the understanding that this would be a worker's government. Much controversy developed afterwards on the actual extent of the workers' rule versus the (communist) party rule in Soviet Russia.

The birth of Soviet Russia also complicated the international scene, posed a challenge to the Allied and the United States, and created shifting alliances with defeated Germany that led to the Rapallo agreement of 1922.

After October 1917, under the complex conditions of civil war and foreign intervention, a new economic system started to emerge which initially gave an important role to the workers' councils/soviets through deliberative assemblies. In that instance, workers retained actual control of the factories until the state under Stalin took over and ultimately dispensed with these bottom-up structures of economic participation and created a bureaucratic structure of economic management.

However, war communism imposed too much hardship on the population, and between 1922 and 1927, it was replaced by the New Economic Policy (NEP), which gave autonomy to private agricultural producers and allowed the price mechanisms and markets to guide food consumption. Private property largely prevailed in rural areas under the NEP.

After the death of Lenin in 1924, heated economic debates developed on the future of the socialist economy with Nicolas Bukharin favouring an extension of the NEP and Yevgeny Preobrazhensky stressing the need for "primitive socialist accumulation" to accelerate growth in the newly created USSR.[10] With the triumph of Stalin in the soviet leadership, a large state bureaucratic apparatus was created to centrally allocate resources to different sectors in the economy (agriculture, industry and services; sectors producing consumer and capital goods) leaving little room for decentralisation, workers' participation and autonomy in the economic realm. The seeds of economic democracy which had existed during the early period of the revolution had vanished (Solimano, 2022).

Keynes visited Russia in 1925 soon after his marriage with Lydia Lopokova, a Russian ballerina. Officially, he represented the University of Cambridge on the bicentenary celebration of the Academy of Sciences, formerly the Imperial Academy of Petersburg. Upon returning, he published his impressions in three articles that first appeared in October of 1925 in the *Nation and Atheneum*, later published by Hogarth Press (founded and run by Leonard and Virginia Wolff of the Bloomsbury group) and included as "A Short View of Russia" in *Essays in Persuasion*. In those articles, JMK analysed the "new faith" of communism and discussed the change in values in Russia away from the pursuit of money-making typical of capitalism; the new goal was working for the community. JMK examined the feasibility and desirability of these new cultural attitudes. He also analysed the principles of the new Soviet economic organisation. In terms of international policy recommendations for the UK, Keynes favoured a loan to Russia to keep the new regime engaged in international trade with the West. The isolation of the new regime was perceived as inconvenient whatever the reasons for that including a displeasure with the decision of the Russians to stop recognising the debts incurred during the Czarist period.

Hyperinflation in Central Europe

The restoration of macroeconomic equilibrium and social balance after WWI was not easy, and extreme monetary instability and explosive inflation affected Germany and Russia and the countries that were dismembered from the Austro-Hungarian empire such as Austria, Poland and Hungary.[11]

The Case of Germany

The most studied case is Germany with classic references being the detailed studies of Graham (1930) and Bresciani-Turroni (1937). At the same time, Keynes in *A Tract on Monetary Reform* spelled with great clarity the use of the inflation tax and illustrated its limitations during episodes of extreme inflation that induced a sharp decline in the demand for money forcing increasing rates of inflation for collecting a certain level of revenue. His analysis uses data from Germany, Russia and Austria during their hyperinflationary periods (see Chapter 3).[12]

A critical year in Germany was 1923 (see Solimano, 1990, 2020). The country suffered an important economic contraction as France occupied the Ruhr, and the economy was hit by hyperinflation. In fact, the price level increased sharply between June 1922 and December 1923. Escalating inflation was accompanied by exorbitant increases in the money supply and even more rapid depreciation of the Reichsmark vis a vis the US dollar and other main international currencies. Hyperinflation sharply diminishes the incentives to produce and invest, and reduces the real value of the money supply and nominal spending, curtailing real economic activity.[13]

The Weimar Republic showed that achieving a consensus between capital and labour and/or among industrialists, financiers and landowners on how to share the cost of the servicing of the public debt acquired during the period 1913–1918, and the war reparations were very difficult – if not impossible – to attain. The resulting political paralysis of this distributive conflict eventually brought very high inflation and other internal economic dislocations. There are at least two schools of thought regarding the causes of the German hyperinflation[14]: one view represented by Graham (1930) is the *balance of payments theory* or passive money school that stresses the fact that war reparations and uncertain external financing led to a very steep deprecia-tion of the German mark that feeds into higher wages and prices, validated by an accommodative monetary policy followed by the Reichsbank (German Central Bank). In this context, money *follows* prices and the exchange rate. The other explanation presented by Bresciani-Turroni (1937) is in line with the *quantity theory of money* stressing the links between money creation and the financing of the fiscal deficit. In this case, the central bank prints money in exchange for bonds issued by the treasury. This is a fiat-money system that re-lies on the legal tender status of paper money unbacked by real assets such as gold for example. In the money-quantity framework, not only money-printing feeds price increases but also an increase in money velocity can contribute to accelerate inflation through a feedback mechanism involving expectations of future inflation. The rise in velocity has as a counterpart a decrease in the de-mand for money as people economise the use of cash balances heavily taxed by high inflation (see Keynes, 2000 [1923], chapter 2). In this situation, the price level grows at a rate above the money supply with the difference being the change in velocity, a fact observed in Germany in 1923. In turn, the lag in tax collection in conditions of very high inflation reduces the real value of tax receipts by the treasury deteriorating the fiscal budget. On the expenditure side, the burden posed by war reparations, debt payments and support spend-ing for social needs also put extra pressure on the budget.

Currencies and Inflation in Soviet Russia

The Russian ruble was a quite stable currency during most of the 19th cen-tury. In the early 1890s, the imperial government's finance minister Sergei Witte implemented monetary reforms that strengthened a ruble-gold parity that lasted until the outbreak of World War I. Thereafter, convertibility was suspended, and the government started to run large fiscal deficits to finance Russia's involvement in World War I. The deficit was covered with money creation leading to the depreciation of the currency in terms of domestic goods and foreign currencies including gold. The imperial government left power in February 1917 substituted by the Kerensky provisional govern-ment that introduced a new currency the "kerenki" that failed to stop infla-tion. In October 1917, the Bolshevik took power replacing the provisional government and suspended in January–February 1918 the servicing of for-eign debt acquired by the imperial and provincial governments. There were several currencies in circulation between 1918 and 1924. During foreign intervention and civil war, various belligerent parties including foreign powers issued their own money that co-existed with the official soviet ruble or *sovznaks*. As of April 1920, around 68 percent of the currency in circulation was constituted by the sovznavks. During war communism and after, there were heated debates on the most adequate monetary regime for Soviet Russia. In 1919–1920, an attempt was made to reduce the use of money and have a barter socialist economy. When the New Economic Policy that reintroduced elements of a market economy was launched in March–August 1921, it was accompanied by a dual monetary system in which a "hard currency", the *chevornetz,* backed by gold co-existed with the paper currency, the sovznaks, that was used in the state sector and rural areas. In 1922, a currency reform was undertaken given the rapid depreciation of the sovznaks. The central bank (Gosbank), the treasury (Narcomfin) and the planning committee (Gosplan) had a say on monetary matters, and controversies on the monetary regime continued. In February 1924, the chevornetz became the only legal tender, and the printing of sovznaks was stopped. In addition, the Soviet government moved to close the fiscal deficit in the fiscal year 1923/1924 and ran a surplus in 1924/1925. This contributed to the stabilisation of the chevornetz in terms of foreign currency and of domestic prices.[15] Given the hostility of foreign powers to the soviet regime, besides the suspension of foreign debt decided in early 1918, no foreign loan supported the stabilisation process undertaken by the Soviet government. Keynes (2000 [1923]) commented that the use of paper rubles was dispensed with altogether at the peak of Russian inflation and replaced by a hard currency tied to sterling and gold. JMK commented that "Russia provides an instructive example (at the least for the moment) of a sound money for substantial transactions along with small change for daily life, the progressive depreciation of which merely represents a quite supportable rate of turn-over tax" (TMR, chapter 2, p. 58).

The Return to the Gold Standard and Stagnation in Britain

The *classic gold standard* before 1913 was an international monetary system based on certain rules obeyed by member countries and rested on two main pillars that were not strictly economic in nature: (a) clear British leadership – through the Bank of England – in international monetary and financial matters and (b) international cooperation among member countries that were on the gold standard that, most generally, played by the rules of the standard. Other prerequisites for the working of the system were price and wage flexibility, limited influence of the labour unions through "wage resistance" and relative isolation of monetary decisions from political considerations. Clearly after WWI, these prerequisites were more a relic of the past.

Despite these realities and calculations of changes in productivity compared with other trade partners, Great Britain decided in 1925 to restore the same 1913 parity (pound sterling price of a unit of gold). There were several rationales for this, among them the intent to restore the pride of an old order, dismissed by the events, through a strong sterling. However, between 1913 and 1923, accumulated inflation and productivity shifts had taken place that affected the competitiveness of the British economy. A result of returning to the parity of 1913 made the pound overvalued, making exports and investment in Britain more expensive abroad. John Maynard Keynes in *The Economic Consequences of Mr. Churchill* noted, vividly, that the new parity was inadequate and would entail a loss of competitiveness for British industry and would contribute to further economic decline in Britain as the export engine would be harmed with adverse consequences on growth, employment and the balance of payments.

In turn, France returned to the gold standard in 1926 under the leadership of President Raymond Poincare but at what is considered as an *undervalued* French franc – just the opposite situation of the UK that *overvalued* the pound.[16] External payment imbalances developed in various countries. However, correcting these imbalances was now different from the hallmark of the classic gold standard prevailing until 1913. The old system was based on an automatic adjustment mechanism that entailed free and unrestricted flows of gold from surplus economies to deficit countries accompanied by rising interest rates (in the deficit country) and falling interest rates (in the surplus country) and prices and wages.

This mechanism was largely absent, however, in the reconstructed gold standard. France, for example, pursued since the mid to late 1920s a policy of building up large reserves of gold that is attributed to have created international deflationary effects as it crowded out available gold reserves in other nations. The automatic adjustment of the balance of payments was no longer operating for various reasons. For example, deflationary adjustment through cuts in wages and transient unemployment became very difficult to accomplish in the environment of stronger labour unions and labour militancy that had emerged after World War I. In addition, the dominance of Great Britain as the main economic power, capital exporter and holder of the global reserve currency, the sterling pound and the critical role played by the Bank of England of the gold standard in the pre-1913 world was clearly diminished. In turn, the United States was not yet prepared, or willing, to take a strong *global* leadership in economic affairs. So, when the clouds of a global recession emerged in the late 1920s, the world was caught in a vacuum of leadership without a clear *hegemon* in place.[17] Keynes was wistful of a strong but still inexperienced Federal Reserve bank in the United States (see *A Tract on Monetary Reform*).

In these circumstances effective cooperation in exchange rate management, orderly capital flows and the possibility of adopting counter-cyclical demand management policies were difficult to achieve. International investors were sensible to uncertainty and searched for safe havens in countries such as the United States. However, between 1930 and 1932, the USA also suffered a series of bank failures showing that the country was not such a financially safe place. Nonetheless, as the political situation in Europe was worsening, capital inflows to the US increased in the mid-1930s.

Until around 1931, several governments still maintained faith in the gold standard and their companion of free convertibility of gold, balanced fiscal budgets and sound money. The conflict with the objectives of high employment and sustained growth was not seen as evident.

War Reparations and American Financing

The fragility of the Weimar Republic and the post-war new equilibrium for Europe was connected to the war reparations agreed by the "Big Four" (Britain, the United States, France and Italy) at the Treatise of Versailles of 1919. The reparations were to compensate the Allied for the damage of the war and could be paid in cash or kind (coal, timber, machinery and so on).

The London Payments schedule in 1921 fixed total reparations at 132 billion gold Marks (the currency of the German empire until 1913 when it was still in the gold standard).

To avoid a socially costly and unpopular contraction in domestic spending to accommodate the foreign transfer associated with war reparations, Germany was borrowing abroad, mainly from New York banks. In fact, in the absence of foreign borrowing, the economy had to generate a big trade surplus (net resource transfer).[18] As it became clear that Germany was unable (or unwilling) to pay the war reparations set by the Allied at Versailles.

At the same time, the United States was not keen on a debilitated Germany and put in place the *Dawes Plan* in 1924 (the name of the plan is after Charles G. Dawes, who was a Director of the US Bureau of the Budget) with the purpose of reschedule payments and, through this mechanism, reduce the burden of war reparations to the German economy. The present value of transfer obligations under the plan is estimated at 59 percent of the German GDP of 1925 (Ritschl, 2005). The implied burden of war reparations under the Dawes Plan was high although, for some, not stifling. However, a few years later, another plan to reduce and stretch out war reparations was again considered: this was the *Young Plan* of 1929/1930; Owen, D. Young was an American industrialist, banker and diplomat who was asked by the US government to look at the sustainability of war reparations in Germany given the exposure of US (and other European) banks to the country.

The value of reparations under the Young plan amounted to 42 percent of the German GDP of 1929, a reduction of 17 percentage points relative to the Dawes plan. The new plan set an annual schedule of payments of 2 billion gold marks for 59 years until 1988. However, the timing of the new Plan was tricky. In Germany, there was no full agreement with it and faced internal opposition by a coalition of conservative parties including the National Socialist Party of Adolf Hitler. The right-wing coalition in Germany challenged the agreement in parliament – the Reichstag – and convened a popular campaign with millions of votes oriented to present a "Liberty Law" against the plan but the proposed law to the Reichstag failed to be approved. Hitler, angrily, despised the event and later, after becoming chancellor in 1933, repelled war reparations altogether by decree.

In turn, the Wall Street Crash of 1929 led US banks to recall lending to Europe, including the commitment made under the Young Plan. This adverse financing development along with the onset of the great depression hit hard the German economy making the servicing of war reparations almost impossible (unemployment rose to 25 percent in 1931 and 32 percent in 1932 and the country was affected by a banking crisis).[19] The US and other allied nations tried to ease the burden on the German economy at the Lausanne Conference of 1932. It was estimated that between 1921 and 1932, Germany had paid nearly 20 million gold marks as war reparations, only 15 percent of the agreed total (nominal) amount of 132 million gold marks or 40 percent of the servicing of bonds A and B.

On the whole, war reparations, even with rescheduling (the Dawes plan) and reparation relief (Young Plan), proved to be economically destabilising for the Weimar Republic and paved the way for the rise of virulent nationalism and steered internal political and social polarisation that led to the rise of national socialism, rearmament and eventually to a new World War.

As already mentioned, John Maynard Keynes had already eloquently alerted and showed with available statistics on the available resources in Germany. According to *The Economic Consequences of Peace,* war reparations, set at too high a level, were to have a crippling effect on the German economy and society. However, there was no universal consensus on the Keynes position. The French economist Etienne Mantoux wrote, during World War II, the book *The Carthaginian Peace or the Economic Consequences of Mr. Keynes* which argues that Keynes drastically *underestimated* the German capacity to pay reparations. In addition, Mantoux doubted that the damage provoked by Germany was the amount determined in the Treaty and considered it much higher. Furthermore, Mantoux not only criticised the statistical analysis of Keynes but also criticised his assessment of the political consequences of the Treaty. In fact, he argued that Keynes' reasoning contributed to create an atmosphere of international leniency and compassion towards Germany that was instrumental to Nazi-led German rearmament in the 1930s and the preparation of a new war of aggression that eventually led to World War II.

Another piece of dissent with Keynes' analysis in *The Economic Consequences of the Peace* came from a book review by Thorsten Veblen (famous for writing *The Leisure Class)*. In the review, Veblen noted that despite the stated focus of the *Economic Consequences* on Germany's capacity to pay war reparations, there was another implicit motivation of the Big Four in the Treatise of Versailles and others to follow (Rapallo, Genoa conferences) oriented to marginalise Soviet Russia to prevent the propagation of communism to Europe and the rest of the world. For Veblen, war reparations had to be analysed jointly in terms of their consequences for both Russia and Germany.

The Great Depression of the 1930s

The Great Depression was an international slump involving a large group of countries both in the core of the capitalist countries (USA and Western Europe) and the European periphery and primary exporters in Latin America, Asia and Australia.

The precise causes of the great depression of the early 1930s remain somewhat of an unresolved mystery in economic analysis and history. There is, probably, not a single cause or a single country responsible for the big international slump. Still we can make the following list of factors that did contribute to the Great Depression: (i) the stock market crash of 1929 in the United States that shaken expectations and destroyed financial wealth, (ii) the decline in terms of trade and capital inflows by exporters of primary products in Latin America and Australia that started in 1928 or before, (iii) a wave of bankruptcies of banks in the early 1930s in America, Austria and Germany, (iv) the deflationary policies pursued by central banks in the context of the gold standard that led to a contraction of effective demand, (v) the timing of abandonment of the gold standard (the evidence seems to show that early exit countries started their recovery sooner), (vi) the fall in domestic prices that increased the real value of debt held by consumers and firms with a negative effect on consumption and investment, and (vii) the lack of a decisive fiscal policy stance, early enough to avoid a large-scale depression (see Solimano, 2020, chapter 4).

Banking Crises

The occurrence of banking crises in several countries of the global north played a significant role in the worsening of the slump. In the United States, there were four waves of panic between 1930 and 1932 in which the public started to withdraw their deposits: in the fall of 1930, in the spring of 1931, in the fall of 1931 and in the fall of 1932 (Romer, 1992). By 1933, 20 percent of the banks that were in operation in 1930 had closed-off operations. Bank runs led these institutions to recall loans reducing the supply of credit to the real sector of the economy. The US Federal Reserve was inactive in providing liquidity when it was needed to avert a banking crisis. The logic of the gold standard prevailed among American policymakers during the Hoover years. In moments of uncertainty that could undermine the exchange rate and the reserves of gold, the money supply was tightened. For example, in response to the sterling crisis of 1931, the Federal Reserve *increased* interest rates at home. Moreover, fiscal authorities following a policy of balanced fiscal budgets increased taxes and reduced fiscal spending, which cut domestic absorption, aggravating the decline in output and the increase in unemployment.

In Vienna in 1929, the Bodencreditanstal, the second most important bank in Austria went under crisis. In 1931, the turn was of Creditanstalt, a main commercial bank in which the Rothschild family had large stakes. The entity failed and had to reorganise with the help of other European banks. This set off a wave of instability on the shilling (Austria's currency) with tremors to the currencies of other Central European economies, including the British pound.[20] In the summer of 1931, a twin banking crisis and currency crisis developed in Germany, which resembled the banking crisis in Austria. In the 1920s, German banks had not been very prudent, over-extending loans to different sectors in an economy affected by large foreign debt obligations (including war reparations) and subject to various shocks to industry. These factors created overall financial fragility that exploded in the 1930s.

Price Deflation

The Great Depression was accompanied by a process of *domestic price deflation*. The overall norm in different countries was a *decline* in the overall price level.[21] In the United States, the Consumer Price Index (CPI) fell by 24 percent between 1929 and 1933, in Canada by 22 percent, in the United Kingdom by 12 percent and in Germany by 27 percent (between 1928 and 1932).

In the periphery of the world economy, between 1929 and 1932 the price level declined by 22 percent in Argentina and by 21 percent in Mexico, and in Australia, prices fell by 17 percent between 1929 and 1931.[22] In Chile, the price level increased by 4 percent between 1929 and 1932.

The macroeconomic effects of price deflation were the subject of controversy and debates among theoretical economists who lived through the era of the Great Depression. Two schools of thought can be identified here. One is the "debt-deflation theory of depressions" identified with the American economist Irving Fisher. This author underscored that a fall in the level of prices tends to *aggravate* a depression as the *real value of debt* held by consumers and firms increases when prices fall. American household debt increased quite substantially during the speculative bubble of the late 1920s. The purchases of stocks were often financed by loans (margins). In the first half of the 1920s, borrowing also increased significantly during the housing market boom, but in this case, loans were oriented to finance the acquisition of housing and land.

Another school of thought predicts that price deflation *increases* the real value of "outside" wealth, particularly the purchasing power of real balances (money). In this case, a decrease in the price level leads to a *positive wealth effect* that can, in principle, counteract the negative effects of price deflation on the real value of liabilities and debt. This "real balance effect" (real government bonds are not "outside wealth") was stressed by the British economist Arthur Cecil Pigou. This is known as "the Pigou effect" (Patinkin, 1948). He argued that an increase in real balances should stimulate consumption, helping to restore aggregate demand and bringing the economy back to full employment (Pigou, 1943).[23]

The Pigou effect, however, was largely dismissed by both John Maynard Keynes and Michael Kalecki.[24] Keynes doubted its empirical relevance as an automatic mechanism to restore full employment in a depressed economy. In turn, Kalecki (in line with Fisher's theory) pointed to the negative impact on the real value of debt servicing of price deflation compressing consumption and investment and thus worsening a depression.

From Depression to Recovery in the United States

A main event leading to the great depression in the United States was the sharp decline in stock market prices of October 1929 that, as explained before, induced a cut in consumption and investment that lasted several years. A negative wealth effect and a squeeze in the supply of credit were the two main financial transmission mechanisms between the financial crash and these two main components of aggregate demand. In addition, the state of the banking system was fragile, and between 1930 and 1932, there were four waves of panic in which depositors started to withdraw their deposits. Bank runs led these institutions to recall loans reducing the supply of credit to the real sector of the economy. The Federal Reserve was inactive in providing liquidity when it was needed to avert a banking crisis. The logic of the gold standard prevailed among American policymakers during the Hoover years. In moments of uncertainty that could undermine the exchange rate and the reserves of gold, the money supply was tightened. For example, in response to the sterling crisis of 1931 in Britain the Federal Reserve *increased* interest rates at home. Moreover, fiscal authorities following a policy of balanced fiscal budgets increased taxes and reduced fiscal spending, which cut domestic absorption, aggravating the decline in output and the increase in unemployment.

The prevailing climate of economic ideas in the period was the doctrine of a strong currency, balanced fiscal budgets and reliance on wage and price flexibility to restore full employment. With the publication of the *General Theory* in 1936, there was a new framework to think in macroeconomics in different terms. The book emphasised as a main cause of the depression a massive failure of aggregate demand that required active fiscal expansion and monetary stimulus (the latter would not work however if the economy was stuck in a "liquidity trap" in which the extra money supply is absorbed by an elastic demand for money thereby keeping interest rates unchanged with no effect on effective demand).

Keynes, observing the actual behaviour of people, emphasised that at times of high uncertainty, individuals increase their demand for money or *preference for liquidity*. This is intuitive: assets such as houses, land, machinery and equipment are *illiquid* and therefore cannot be easily transformed into cash when needed. Between 1929 and 1933, the money stock fell by 31 percent and did not accommodate an increase in the demand for money (e.g. fall in money-velocity) with the predictable effect of depressing nominal spending.

President Hoover defended the gold standard parity (a strong dollar) until the end of his mandate, undertook contractionary monetary policies and pursued a policy of balanced fiscal budgets. In contrast, F.D. Roosevelt abandoned this orthodox policy stance (FDR was elected in December 1932 and inaugurated in March of 1933). Roosevelt declared a nationwide "bank holiday" on 6 March 1933, closed all banks and allowed them to reopen only those considered as solvent by Federal inspectors. In addition, Roosevelt became convinced that the fixed parity of the gold standard was a straitjacket. After abandoning the cherished gold standard, and devaluing the US dollar against the Canadian dollar and European currencies (Edwards, 2018). There was more space for undertaking expansionary policies. In addition, FDR pursued a "reflationary" policy of money creation to increase prices and stimulate economic activity.

Devaluing the exchange rate gave Roosevelt room to experiment with active demand management policies, something that was probably not feasible under the parity of the gold standard. The policies of the New Deal included the launching of the National Industrial Recovery Act (NIRA), the Agricultural Adjustment Act (AAA) oriented to support prices of agricultural goods to help farmers and production to recover. To strengthen confidence in the banking system, a Federal Deposit Insurance Corporation was created. Policies oriented to boost economic recovery and financial stability were supplemented by the creation of a nationwide social security system to help alleviate the social consequences of unemployment and provide old age security.

These policies and reforms represented a major reorientation in the priorities of economic policy in America towards objectives of economic growth, full employment and social insurance. It was a truly "regime change" away from the priorities of the Hoover administration oriented to defending the value of the dollar and balancing the budget (although fiscal policy under Roosevelt, properly measured, was not that active).

After four years of economic contraction between 1930 and 1933, a recovery took place from 1934 to 1936, interrupted by a new recession in 1937–1938. According to MIT professor Cary Brown (Brown, 1940), after 1933 fiscal policy in the US was not clearly expansionary when evaluated at different levels of government (see also Romer 1990, 1992). The whole cycle of depression and recovery (lasting 11 years) was only completed in 1940 when the peak of 1929 in per capita GDP was reached again.

The Recovery in Europe

The economic slump in Britain was less severe and of shorter duration than the contraction in the US, Germany, Canada and Austria. However, employment contracted in coal-mining activities, in the steel sector, cotton, shipyard building and the working classes underwent serious human suffering. Unemployment reached nearly 20 percent of the workforce during the slump and exports, in value, contracted by nearly 50 percent. The social reality of the British at the time of the great depression was depicted vividly by George Orwell in his book *The Road to Wigan Pier*.

The depression in Britain had domestic causes but it was also related to the slump in the US and the banking crisis in Austria and Germany in 1931 that affected the value of the British pound. Like the US , Britain tried first orthodox policies of balancing the fiscal budget, increasing taxes and cutting spending during the depression but this added additional contractionary pressures to the economy. However, in September 1931, the UK abandoned the gold standard and devalued the sterling. This was nearly *two years before the United States*. The depreciation of the pound allowed Britain to implement expansive monetary policies to spur economic growth and reduce unemployment. In 1932, Neville Chamberlain who had become chancellor after the elections of 1931 introduced tariffs on agricultural and industrial goods but exempted imports from the countries belonging to the British Commonwealth. It is unclear, however, that protectionism was expansionary if international effects on the export side were taken into consideration. In any case, the recovery of economic activity in Britain started in 1932, and in 1937–1939, the output was 18 percent above its level of 1929.[25]

Sweden and Norway also abandoned the gold standard and devalued their currencies in September 1931 and Denmark in November 1931 devalued its currency and Finland did so in December 1931. The Nordic countries followed the lead of Britain and opted out of gold.

We mentioned before that leaving the gold standard earlier facilitated the economic recovery after the slump of 1929–1933, and this was the case of the UK and the Nordics. The United States remained in the gold standard until early 1933 and the "gold block countries" (France, Belgium, and Switzerland) until 1935–1936. Germany and Italy introduced foreign exchange controls in 1931 and used that device to defend their parities relative to gold for a while, in a sort of disguised membership to the gold standard regime. Of course, this was a faked allegiance as the gold standard implied the free convertibility of gold being incompatible with practices of currency inconvertibility.

In the 1920s, France was busy trying to obtain war reparations from Germany, an often unsuccessful endeavour. France managed to grow at a respectable average annual 3.5 per capita between 1919 and 1929 but contracted at a – 0.3 percent per year between 1930 and 1939. The country suffered from exchange rate instability and inflation in the first half of the 1920s but as noted before the franc was stabilised in 1926 by President Raymond Poincare. Interestingly, France, unlike other countries, avoided a financial crisis in the first half of the 1930s. Still, economic troubles were not absent and ultimately triggered political effects favouring the *Front Populaire* (Popular Front) of the socialist leader Leon Blum who was elected in 1936. Economic growth was modest in 1936–1939 in France.

Macroeconomic (and political) development in Germany in the 1920s was driven, largely, by the need to make a foreign resource transfer abroad (war reparations of the Versailles Treaty and sanctioned by the London schedule in 1921) as we analysed in the previous section.

The US government supported the Dawes Plan of 1924 and the Young Plan of 1929. However, things turned more complicated when the US Federal Reserve Bank increased interest rates to cool off speculation in the stock market and reduced international lending in 1928. This shattered market confidence in the German economy that was crucially dependent on US loans to serve its foreign obligations. In addition, German exports were affected by the Hawley-Smoot tariff levied on imports imposed by the United States in 1930. The economic crisis led to a sharp rise in unemployment from around 650,000 people in 1928 to over 3 million in 1930, climbing further to 6 million in early 1933.

In 1931, a banking crisis affected the German currency, the Reichsmark. Like the US under Hoover, Germany followed an orthodox policy of balancing the budget, reduced spending and salaries, and increased interest rates. The internally polarised political situation left little room for consensus on a stabilisation programme that could deal realistically with Germany's debt overhang problems. As said, when Hitler took power, he suspended all reparation payments and controlled labour unions but increased public spending particularly military spending (see Solimano, 2020). These policies allowed Germany to experience a steady economic recovery from 1933 to 1939 along with a substantial decline in unemployment under the guidance of Hjalmar Schacht appointed in charge of the German economy by the Fuhrer. Schacht abandoned his previous orthodoxy of the 1920s when he headed the German central bank and undertook policies of state intervention, de-linking with international markets and massive public works to pull Germany out of the depression. Economic nationalism and autarky formed the cornerstone of Nazi economic policies helped by Schacht and his good connections with the business community inside and outside Germany, besides his prestige in stabilising the mark in the 1920s.[26]

Notes

1 This chapter partly draws on material from Chapters 3 and 4 of Solimano (2020).
2 See Solimano (2010).
3 Analysis of inequality in that period includes Hatton and Williamson (2005).
4 Eloranta (2007, 2013).
5 These figures are taken from Table 2.1 in Feinstein, Temin and Tonolio (2008). Also, Rockoff (2005).
6 We do have data of cuts in military spending after 1918 only for the US and the UK. Britain sharply reduced its defence spending to GDP ratio from 32 percent in 1918 to 13 percent in 1919 and further to 4 percent in 1920 and the United States cut military expenditure from 13 percent of GDP in 1918 to 3 percent in 1920.
7 Pindyck and Solimano (1993) calculate the value of *waiting* for irreversible investment under uncertainty.
8 The end of the Austro-Hungarian empire after WWI gave rise to six successor states: Austria, Hungary (both ending up much diminished in both territory and population), Czechoslovakia, Poland, Romania and Yugoslavia.
9 See Gramsci (1920 [1968]).
10 Preobrazhensky (1926).
11 Hungary also experienced again a very virulent hyperinflation in 1946 and Greece in the first half of the 1940s (Palairet, 2000).
12 Other inflation analyses include Sargent (1982), Dornbusch and Fischer (1986) and Végh (1992).
13 According to Maddison (2013), per capita German GDP fell by 17 percent in 1923, the peak year of inflation. Other estimates provide a range of output decline in *real national income* that year between 10 percent and 24 percent (Solimano, 2020).
14 Analysis of German hyperinflation of 1922–1923 can be found in Graham (1930) favouring the passive money school and Bresciani-Turroni (1937) supporting the quantity theory approach. Solimano (1991) offers an international perspective on this and other Central European hyperinflationary episodes.
15 See Katzenellebaum (1925) and Nenovsky (2015).
16 Feinstein, Temin and Tonolio (2008) and Eichengreen (1992).
17 Kindleberger (1973 [2013]) underscored the importance of the lack of a hegemony power due to the combination of British decay and the still unconsolidated American emergence as a top of economic power.
18 The effect of war reparations and their financing gave rise to various exchanges between J.M. Keynes and Swedish economist B. Ohlin on the "transfer problem".
19 The Nazis in power put in place a command economy, undertook large employment programs and rearmament that stimulated internal economy activity in such a way that by 1938 the unemployment rate was only 2.2 percent, see Ritschl (2005).
20 Good descriptions of these banking crises are in Feinstein, Temin and Tonolio (2008), James (2002) and Eichengreen (1992).
21 Chile was an exception as it recorded positive, but low, inflation in the years of the big depression.
22 Twoney (1983).
23 Pigou (1943).
24 Kalecki (1944).
25 Output in the United States in 1937–1939 was only 3 percent above the level of 1929.
26 See Frieden (2007, Chapter 9) and Chapter 3.

3   *A Tract on Monetary Reform.* The Evil of Inflation and the Management of Money and Foreign Exchanges

Introduction

The *Tract* is a book that deals with issues of money, prices, exchange rates and monetary policy in a world different from the gold standard. Historically, it covers the period 1913–1923. It deals with the social consequences of inflation (a steady rise in the price level) both in terms of redistribution of incomes between debtors and creditors, workers and capitalists. It also considers the economic impacts of changes in the value of money on employment, production and investment as economic calculation in a monetary capitalist economy is impaired by changes in the value of the means of transaction and the common denominator of contracts. Keynes reflected that inflation becomes a disruptive disease that affects the working of the economic body and harms prosperity. The *Tract* discusses inflation during WWI and its aftermath.

JMK notes that inflation was a sort of new malaise and people, and institutions were unprepared to deal with it. In the 19th century and early 20th century (pre-1913), inflation had largely disappeared.

Monetary reform, a topic of the TMR, has a long history. The Bullionist debates, the controversies between the banking school and the currency school, and the debates on bimetallism in the last third of the 19th century and the functioning of the gold standard in the early 20th century, particularly its sensitivity to the discoveries of gold deposits on the money supply and prices in countries that were tied to gold and the role of central banks in counteracting these disturbances coming from abroad. The *Treaty* focuses on the objectives and instruments of monetary policy in coordination with commercial banks in countries that enjoy a degree of national autonomy in the conduct of monetary policy.

The *Tract* is, essentially, a collection of edited articles that Keynes had written before, mostly for *The Manchester Guardian Commercial*, a British newspaper specialised in economic and financial matters. The book also included edited material coming from Keynes' own lecture notes of courses on money that he had taught at Cambridge University since around 1911.

DOI: 10.4324/9781003480785-3

The social structure in the *Tract* is composed of several segments of society: rentiers, debtors, investors, businessmen and entrepreneurs, and the working class. They face different consequences when the *value of money* changes unexpectedly depending on their net asset or debt position and whether their incomes derived from selling labour efforts and/or holding financial assets are fixed in nominal terms. In this context, some people benefit from inflation while others are harmed by it. On the other side of the coin, deflation (a process of decline in the price level) can be costly in terms of output, employment and investment and has also redistributive effects.

The book was written at a time in which several economies of Europe such as Germany, Austria, Hungary, Poland and Russia were affected by rampant inflation in countries in which fiscal deficits were large, balance of payments was weak and central banks (or state banks) were financing with the printing of money to cover large fiscal deficits. Currencies were generally weak due to war reparations payments, lack of foreign hard currencies and fragile balance of payments positions (see Chapter 2).

What happens when governments resort to the inflation tax to cover fiscal deficits? What are the limits and consequences of the use of the inflation tax? were questions that JMK tried to answer. The main policy concern of the book is on how to stabilise the value of money by actions of governments and institutions rather than as a natural, spontaneous consequence of the function of the economic system. Analytically, the book adopts the quantity theory of money (QTM) as the main framework but as already mentioned in Chapter 1 does not adhere to a rigid, orthodox view of a dominant causality from the money supply to prices. Keynes, with an eye on the *demand for money* rather than the supply, stressed the effects of changes in habits and norms by the public and banks concerning their liquidity policy. As mentioned in Chapter 1, Keynes was inclined to an accommodative monetary policy oriented to price stability that adjusted to changes in the demand for money. A change from active money policy to somewhat of a passive money stance is advocated in normal circumstances. This precludes, of course, accommodating a *large* fiscal deficit by printing money as this could lead to very high inflation.

The book focuses on critical questions of monetary policy and underscores the uneasy choices that governments and monetary authorities faced in the context of high inflation after WWI and the breakdown of the classic gold standard: should the price level (domestic value of money) or the exchange rate (external value of money) be stabilised? What should be the relevant standard for a stable value of money: commodities, foreign goods or gold? If observed exchange rates are misaligned with respect to equilibrium values given by the doctrine of purchasing power parity should the realignment take place through currency devaluation or the deflation of domestic prices? Is it wise and feasible to restore the pre-1914 gold standard in the new economic and geopolitical realities of the early 1920s? How monetary policy be conducted to ensure internal price stability in the context of floating exchange rates and erratic inflation? These are critical questions that JMK seeks to address in the *Tract*.

The historical period between 1913 and 1923 affected England, Europe, the United States and other nations in ways discussed in more detail in Chapter 2.

Effects of Price Inflation (and Deflation)

Chapter 1 of the TMR is devoted to "The Consequences of Changes in the Value of Money". The inflation rate in the period 1913–1923 was over 59 percent in Britain, 311 percent in France, 482 percent in Italy, 765,000 percent in Germany, 57 percent in the USA and 79 percent in India. In some countries, most of the increases took place in 1913–1919, but in Germany, the process of rapid price increases started gathering momentum in 1920–1921 getting to extreme levels in 1922–1923.

The environment of monetary stability of the good old days (pre 1913) allowed the development of financial instruments such as the gilt, a bond issued by the British government that never had defaulted on its public debt and therefore enjoyed high credibility among investors. Savers could be confident in the stability and safety of the value of the currency on which contracts of delivery of payments to a future date were denominated. This tranquil and predictable economic environment was upset by rapid price increases associated with generalised excess demand during the war and the monetisation of fiscal deficits that took place in some countries in the years after the armistice was signed.

The TMR notes that the irruption of inflation found society *unprepared* to deal with a process of rising prices. Existing habits and inertia prevail and are not immediately modified. The redrawing of financial and labour contracts incorporating an inflation premium was not a common practice at the time.

The appearance of inflation disrupted the functioning of the economy as most spot transactions of goods and for future delivery are denominated in official money, typically, a legal tender. A message of the book is that *unexpected changes* in the value of money affect the real value of money contracts and produce undesired redistributions of income and wealth. The *Tract* identifies at least three social groups affected – with some gaining and others losing – by the changes in the value of money:

1 The Investment Class (rentiers often earning a fixed interest rate)
2 The Business Class (producers, entrepreneurs with free prices)
3 The Earner (workers and employees with fixed salaries)

The Investment Class are typically people who buy stocks, bonds, mortgages and so on. Inflation affects the value of their investments by eroding the purchasing power of the principal invested and the real value of interest payments. As said, after a long period of relative stability in prices, the money interest rate of a bond does *not* incorporate compensation for expected price increases (inflation). In contrast, inflation benefits the government and farmers when both entities have acquired debts. The government issues public debt to finance public spending, particularly during wartime. Farmers and agriculturalists often borrow to finance their acquisitions of land, build their houses and finance working capital. In an inflationary environment, the real value of their debt, including debt servicing, was reduced by inflation.

Inflation, however, is not an unmitigated blessing for governments. In a context of high inflation, the real value of taxes that represent the revenues of the state tends to decline with inflation, due to the existence of a time lag in tax collection. This has been labelled the *Keynes-Olivera-Tanzi effect*. Inflation also can affect relative prices: for example, the evolution of the price of food and agricultural products may differ from the changes in the general price level.

The inflation that deals the *Tract* is largely unexpected or unanticipated. Keynes is certainly aware that the *expectation* of future inflation is what matters in contracting a loan or drawing a salary contract. However, he was also mindful that there was substantial inertia and institutional rigidities to adapt the contract structure in loans, wages, housing rents and so on to the appearance of inflation since 1913 in England and Europe more generally.

Nowadays, countries with a long inflationary history, typically in Latin America, have learned to develop indexation mechanisms applied to wage contracts, the payment of house rents, loan dividends and interest rates, thereby largely avoiding redistributions of income or wealth due to inflation. But, this was not the case in Europe in the 1910s and 1920s.

The "Business Class" is composed of "merchants and manufacturers", and the entrepreneurs *benefit* from price increases. The value of sales, inventories and goods-in-process go up with inflation. In addition, if the entrepreneur has borrowed money to expand its capital equipment and build structures, it will benefit from inflation as a debtor as loans may not be indexed to prices.

Regarding the wage earner, the presumption is that he/she tends to benefit in this environment of price increases as it probably, taking advantage of the strengthened bargaining power of labour gained after the war, managed to get higher wages. However, at a more general level, it is recognised that the existence of lags between the occurrence of price increases and the readjustment of wages and salaries.

As a general conclusion, JMK states that:

> We conclude that Inflation redistributes wealth in a manner very injurious to the investor, very beneficial to the businessman, and probably, in modern industrial conditions, beneficial on the whole to the [wage] earner. Its most striking consequence is its *injustice* to those who in good faith have committed their savings to titles of money rather than to things.

> ... the diminution in the production of wealth which has taken place in Europe since the war has been, to a certain extent, at the expense, not of consumption but of the accumulation of capital. Moreover, inflation has not only diminished the capacity of the investing class to save but has destroyed the atmosphere of confidence which is a condition of the willingness to save. Yet a growing population requires for the maintenance of the same standard of living, a proportionate growth of capital.
>
> (TMR, pp. 30–31)

These comments underscore that inflation has not only a redistributive effect but also penalises savings, capital formation and economic growth due to the loss of confidence in the value of savings and the uncertainty on the future return on investment.

Commenting on the costs associated with both inflation and deflation:

> We see, therefore, that rising prices and falling prices each have their characteristic disadvantages. The Inflation which causes the former means injustice to individuals and to classes particularly to investors; and is therefore unfavourable to savings. The Deflation which causes falling prices means Impoverishment to labour and to enterprise by leading *entrepreneurs* to restrict production, in their endeavour to avoid losses to themselves, and it's therefore disastrous to employment. The counterparts are, of course, also true—namely that deflation means Injustice to borrowers and that Inflation leads to the over-stimulation of industrial activity.
>
> ...
>
> Thus, Inflation is unjust, and Deflation is inexpedient. Of the two, perhaps Deflation is, if we exclude exaggerated inflations such as that of Germany, the worse, because it is worse, in an impoverished world, to provoke unemployment than to disappoint the *rentier*. But it is not necessary that we should weigh one evil against the other. It is easier to agree that both are evils to be shunned. The Individualistic Capitalism of to-day, precisely because it entrusts savings to the individual investor and the individual employer, presumes a stable measuring -rod of value and cannot be efficient –perhaps cannot survive—without one.
>
> (TMR, p. 40)

Keynes considers that both inflation and deflation are *arbitrary processes* in the sense of delinking incomes and wealth from conscious effort and ingenuity of the individual as the change in the value of money is an *extraneous force* beyond the control of the borrower, debtor, entrepreneur or wage earner. For JMK, small or moderate inflation is a lesser evil than deflation and recession but urges not to conform with either of them. Governments should strive for price stability avoiding either (significant) inflation or deflation. Nonetheless, it is unclear from reading the *Tract* what would be a concrete threshold beyond which inflation becomes problematic.

In this context, in light of the consequences of inflation and deflation, JMK advocates for the:

> regulation of the standard of value to be subject of *deliberate action*. We can no longer afford to leave it in the category of which the distinguishing characteristics are possessed in different degrees by the weather, the birth-rate, and the constitution-matters which are settled by natural causes or are the resultant of the separate action of many individuals acting independently or require a Revolution to change them.

Not much faith is put on a laissez-faire or spontaneous solution to the problem of inflation/deflation.

Textbox: Irving Fisher: The US Parallel to JMK

Among the greatest economists of the first half of the 20th century, we find the US economist Irving Fisher (1867–1947). He made important contributions to general equilibrium analysis parallel to Leon Walras and utility analysis that also presented the results of Edgeworth and Pareto. That work was presented in the publication of Fisher's PhD Thesis at Yale University in 1892 (he was the first ever to receive such a degree in economics from Yale). He was one of the modern fathers of the modern quantity theory of money, or "monetarism". His main books in that respect were *Appreciation and Interest* (1896), *The Rate of Interest* (1907) and *The Purchasing Power of Money* (1911). This work influenced in important ways the writing of *The Tract* by Keynes.

Fisher's quantity theory of money equation (called the "Yale" version, given his university affiliation) preceded the Marshall and Pigou Cambridge version by many years.

Fisher's QTM equation was predicated on the concept of exchange, where money supply times velocity equaled price level times the *volume of monetary transactions, or T.*

Fisher also addressed the price level in monetarist theory later in *The Purchasing Power of Money*, 1911, and suggested that investors and savers were hampered by "money illusion" – that is, they couldn't differentiate correctly between changes in nominal money from changes in its purchasing power (real money).

As a way towards stabilising prices (against inflation and deflation), he derived what he called a "compensated dollar plan" to stabilise the value of money against the price level predicated on gold conversion for determining money value.

Another field in which Fisher made important contributions was interest rate analysis and capital theory exposed in Fisher's *The Nature of Capital and Income*, 1906; expanded upon in *The Rate of Interest*, 1907; and encapsulated in *The Theory of Interest*, 1930.

Fisher called interest "an index of a community's preference for a dollar of present [income] over a dollar of future income". He labelled his theory of interest the "impatience and opportunity" theory, as blended time preference between income (or consumption) today and tomorrow and the opportunity to invest savings in physical or financial assets to obtain a return in the future.

A very important contribution of Fisher was distinguishing between *nominal* interest rate and the *real* interest rates. He conjectured that the nominal interest rate – that is, the one that is stated and observed in the marketplace – differs from the real interest rate because it doesn't capture the effect of inflation as a measure of the increase in the price level. Only when the inflation rate *expected* by the public is subtracted from the nominal interest rate can the real interest be approximated. This is known as the "Fisher equation".

Irving Fisher also wrote about Index Numbers, promoted econometric analysis and helped to establish the Econometric Society with Ragnar Frisch in the early 1930s. He also wrote on "the debt deflation theory of depressions" (Fisher, 1933), in which the increase in the real value of debt held by households and firms makes it more difficult to serve those debts hampering the balance sheets of banks that react by curtailing credit and selling assets provoking a contraction in economic activity. Fisher wrote not only on economics but also on health, the good life, alcohol prohibition, peace and other topics.

Both Irving Fisher and John Maynard Keynes were active players in the stock market (in the USA and UK). Each of them made a good fortune early on in speculating in the stock market. Each of them also lost a good fortune with the Stock Market Crash in 1929.

Before the Crash, Irving Fisher had become a popular, weekly US guru-writer for the media on financial strategy during the Roaring Twenties, predicated largely on his "trend"-knowledge of statistics and index numbers underlying the stock market.

Unfortunately, just two weeks before the Crash, Fisher wrote in the *New York Times* those stocks had reached "a new and *permanently* high plateau."

Again, both the Gambler Fisher and the Gambler JMK lost a lot of money when the Dow Jones crashed. JMK recouped his losses. Fisher did not.

Inflation Tax and Public Finances

Chapter 2 of the TMR is devoted to "Public Finance and Changes in the Value of Money" and alerts that inflation is a (largely disguised) *method of taxation* used by governments:

A Government can live for a long time, even the German Government or the Russian Government by printing paper money. That is to say, it can by this means secure the command over real resources, --resources just as real as those obtained by taxation.

(TMR, p. 41)

A suggestive, neat, calculation of the logic and magnitude of the inflation tax is provided in the following terms:

Let us suppose that there are 9,000,000 currency notes, and they have altogether a value equivalent to 36,000,000 gold dollars. Suppose the government prints a further 3,000,000 notes so that the amount of currency is now 12,000,000; then in accordance with the above theory [Quantity Theory of Money], the 12,000,000 notes are still only equivalent to $ 36,000,000. In the first state of affairs, therefore each note =$ 4, and in the second state of affairs each note=$3. Consequently the 9,000,000 notes held by the public are now worth $ 27,000,000 instead of $ 36,000,000. Thus, by the process of printing additional notes the Government has transferred from the public to itself an amount of resources equal to $ 9,000,000 just as successfully as if it had raised this sum in taxation. Of whom has the tax fallen? Clearly on the holders of the original 9,000,000 motes, whose notes are now worth 25 percent less than they were before. The inflation tax has amounted to a tax of 25 percent on all holders of notes in proportion to their holdings. The burden of the tax is well spread, cannot be evaded, costs nothing to collect and falls, in a rough sort of way, in proportion to the wealth of the victim. No wonder its superficial advantages have attracted Ministers of Finance.

(TMR, p. 43)

For a given purchasing power of money in terms of gold dollars (the command on real resources), Keynes shows that by printing more currency notes, the government will *not alter* the total gold value of money – its purchasing power in terms of metallic – but the value of existing notes will *depreciate* in terms of gold (as prices rise in proportion to the increase in the stock of currency notes). A main conclusion is that a government by printing more money will manage to extract real resources from the public like any other tax.

However, this tax is *unconventional* and has some appealing advantages over traditional taxation: it is costless to collect and cannot be evaded, its burden incidence is more widespread than traditional taxes and the base on which the tax is excised is the stock of currency in circulation. Several of the shortcomings of conventional taxation can be circumvented by using the inflation tax.

Once discovering this seemingly marvellous method of taxation, Keynes asks whether it can be used at will by a government, say without apparent restrictions, given its apparent conveniences? As this method is used, mostly, in contexts of very high inflation, the answer is negative. The experience of hyperinflation in Germany, Austria and Russia shows, eloquently, its eventual limits.

The mechanics of the tax incidence are not uniform. Initially, unexpectedly high inflation can produce some inefficient reactions by the public: they may want to postpone buying goods in the expectation that inflation will be transient; for this purpose, they may hoard *more* money which will increase the burden of the inflation tax. As time goes on and people perceive inflation is high and/or escalating, they tend to react in, at least, three ways to avoid being taxed by rapid price increases:

1   Buying durable, physical, objects such as jewellery, furniture and art that are assets that, in general, tend to protect against the depreciation of the currency.
2   Increasing the turnover of existing cash balances to avoid experiencing losses from rising prices. People will increase the frequency of purchases, say over a week or so, passing cash from hand to hand, more quickly. In other terms, there will be an increase in the *velocity of circulation of money.*
3   Using foreign money – "hard currencies" – rather than the depreciated local money to carry out transactions.

Therefore, these three responses *tend to reduce the demand for money, shifting* the portfolios of the public from notes and demand deposits (checking accounts) to inflation-proof assets. Another way to look at this is an *increase* in the *velocity of circulation* of money. As the money stock in the hands of the public – the tax base – is reduced, increasing rates of inflation are needed to collect the same real resources for the government.

The dynamics is such that as inflation escalates to ever higher levels, the demand for money shrinks and the economy is *demonetised*. At this point, the new method of taxation – the inflation tax – proves to be very inefficient and costly. At very high rates of the inflation tax, the conveniences of using money – compared to the direct barter of goods and services – disappear; the contract structure of the economy (for goods, labour, financial instruments) expressed in money collapses since an implicit requisite – the constancy of the value of money – vanishes. A well-functioning monetary economy relies on a network of contracts expressed in monetary terms. If the value of money changes because of inflation or deflation, the efficiency of the contract system declines with adverse consequences. Keynes, cautiously, attributed to Lenin in *The Economic Consequences of the Peace* (Keynes, 1971 [1920]) saying that inflation or the debasement of money was an effective way to destroy the capitalist system. However, it seems that Lenin was also aware of the negative consequences of inflation and the excessive printing of paper money for workers and the overall economy in an article entitled "The Impending Catastrophe" of September 1917 just one month before the outbreak of the October revolution and still during the Kerensky government.[1]

Hyperinflation leads to a complete destruction of the value of the currency. This obviously penalises production and employment collapses. Furthermore, the public finances of the government deteriorate at very high rates of inflation as taxes are collected in a very depreciated currency: the new method of taxation becomes self-defeating for the government when used in excess. The illusory feature of having found a costless method of taxation proves its futility.

It is an empirical regularity that hyperinflation tends not to last more than say 9–18 months before they are stabilised as it happened in Germany, Austria and Russia in 1922–1923 and other historical cases. The ruin of an economic system affected by explosive inflation, inclusive of public finances based on conventional taxation, is so severe that it becomes urgent to stabilise prices.

Keynes calculates, drawing from the experiences of Russia, Germany and Austria, that rates of inflation around 100 percent every three months – equivalent to a *daily rate* of inflation of slightly more than 1 percent – still deliver a substantial revenue from the inflation tax. However, if rates of inflation exceed that level, the economy approaches a situation close to the virtual disappearance of the use of money as a means of transaction and unit of value.

In the case of Russia, the adoption of a currency fully backed by sterling and gold – the chevornetz – circulating along with a weak currency, the sovznak led to a dual currency system in which a stable currency (chevornetz) was used for large transactions and the weak currency was used for small transaction. The "bad money" also was the base for the inflation tax, now at more moderate levels.

The *Tract* identifies three options available to a country to escape from a severe deterioration of public finances and high public debt:

1   A repudiation of internal debt
2   Inflationary erosion of debt (principal and the flow of interest payments)
3   A capital levies

Regarding the first method of simply not paying debt obligations, JMK says:

> The first is Repudiation. But except as accompaniment of Revolution, this method is too crude, too deliberate, and too obvious in its incidence. The victims are immediately aware and cry out too loud, so that, in the absence of revolution, this solution may be ruled out as regards *internal* debt, in Western Europe.
>
> (TMR, p. 64)

Concerning the second method "Currency Depreciation which becomes Devaluation when it is fixed and confirmed by law", it was adopted in the countries that emerged from WWI and amounted to a reduction of the real burden of the (national) debt in a magnitude of 50–100 percent; in Germany, bondholders lost most of their holding in real terms; in France, the depreciation of debt was estimated by Keynes in around one-third with respect to a counterfactual of a stable franc; and in Italy, the loss is estimated in one-quarter. In this method, small savers suffer but entrepreneurs are bound to gain due to windfall profits. In general, rentiers and holders of fixed income assets tend to be affected.

Regarding a Capital Levy – inheritance taxes ("death duties"), income taxes, taxes of unearned income – the *Tract* consigns that its application on a large scale is dubious, although it is recognised as a "rational, deliberate method". Comparing the Currency Depreciation (inflation) with the Capital Levy, the former is indiscriminate as affects those holding cash balances and all contracts denominated in money; in contrast, a capital levy is more targeted, focused and less arbitrary. There are several trade-offs or dilemmas in the way fiscal imbalances are reduced and the national debt is brought to more reasonable levels as a share of national income. The claims of debt holders must be compared with the willingness to pay taxes by the population. Reducing a fiscal deficit can be costly. There is no such a thing as an "uncovered deficit". Inflation by transferring real resources from the public to the government is equivalent to more conventional taxes "such as beer-duty and income taxes although the costs of administration, incidence, ability to evade and reach are different".

Devaluation and capital levy are often attacked, admits Keynes, as they go against "the sanctity of contracts" under which capitalism is based. However,

JMK admits that the right of the individual to repudiate contracts has to be balanced by the right of the state to control vested interest for the common good. Usury and intolerable inequalities may require reneging contracts or "the absolutists of contract …will be the father of revolution".

The Quantity Theory of Money (QTM) and Exchange Rate Determination

This Chapter 3 focuses on the theory of money and the theory of foreign exchanges. It is important to recognise that money does not derive utility or satisfaction in itself. The utility of using money is *indirect* and is associated with the services and conveniences it renders and the purchasing power it entails. These basic properties of money are further underscored in *A Treatise on Money* (Chapter 4 of this book).

In addition, the demand for cash balances depends on habits and customs related to the frequencies of payments and the receipt of salaries and other sources of income. Traditionally, people use notes, coins and cheques drawn on current accounts in the banking system. In modern times, people pay for goods and services, and they acquire them with debit and credit cards. Unlike a century ago, nowadays, the use of cash and cheques is sharply declining in many countries and is replaced by digital money such as credit cards, electronic bank transfers, cryptocurrencies and so on.

At the time of writing of the *Tract*, the dominant theory of money was the quantity theory that can be presented in at least two variants:

1 As a relation between the money in circulation (stock of money multiplied by the velocity of circulation) and the *value of spending in consumption goods* (a bundle of consumption goods times a price index of the consumption bundle). In other words, both cash and cheques are held in a certain proportion of expenditure in consumption.
2 As a relation between the money in circulation and the *number of transactions* carried out in the economy in a unit of time. Money is held in proportion to the value of transactions a person or firm must undertake.

The first formulation – often referred to as the "Cambridge Equation" – is associated, sometimes using the terminology of "volume of resources", with Pigou and Marshall and is the formulation preferred by Keynes. The second specification – the "Yale Equation" – was adopted by Irving Fisher.

In the Pigou-Marshall-Keynes formulation, people maintain a certain proportion of money in cash (notes) and another proportion in the form of cheques to consume. In turn, commercial banks define a certain percentage of their deposits in the form of cash to stand ready to meet the liquidity requirements of their clients.

In the *Tract,* the formula for the quantity theory equation is expressed as:

$$n = p\left(k + rk'\right) \tag{3.1}$$

in which:

n = money in circulation

p = price index of consumption goods

k = value of consumption units (bundle) held in cash

k' = value of consumption units (bundle) held in current accounts at the banks against cheques

r = proportion of deposits (liabilities) held in cash by the banks

If k, r and k' are constant, then there is a direct proportionality between money in circulation and the price level. In the orthodox interpretation of the QTM, the dominant causality runs from money to prices. An increase in the supply of money of x percent increases prices in x percent provided the demand for money/velocity remains constant.

However, Keynes rejects this simple interpretation of the QTM and offers a richer formulation noting that preferences for holding liquidity in the form of cash or cheques may change over time as well as the preference of banks regarding how much of their liabilities (deposits) are held in cash to meet the liquidity claims of their clients.

According to JMK, the constancy of the k, k' and r parameters assumed by the rigid adherents of the QTM is unwarranted. Also, central banks can induce commercial banks to adjust their cash reserves through changes in the discount rate (the cost of advancing liquidity to the banks in exchange for bills and commercial paper). The values of k and k' depend on the convenience of holding cash and cheques for carrying out transactions. According to the *Tract,* around 10–20 percent of people's incomes are customarily held in money balances. Nonetheless, there is an opportunity cost of holding resources in the form of liquid assets versus buying a bond or acquiring shares of a company that yield an interest or pay a dividend. JMK also makes the subtle, but relevant point, that k and k' may *not be independent of n* (the supply of money in circulation). For example, an increase in the money supply associated with an inflow of gold from abroad – i.e. the discovery of gold in South Africa and increased shipments to England at the turn of the 20th century may lead to the Bank of England to induce commercial banks through changes in the discount rate to raise the proportion of deposits held in cash as the cost of borrowing for the banks increase. The aim of the monetary authorities is to moderate the "credit cycle", say expansions and contractions of the level of economic activity correlated to increases or decreases in the stock of credit provided by the banks.

The picture that emerges from the *Tract* is of complex interactions between factors such as the money supply, changes in the monetary habits of the public and business affecting the demand for money, policies of the central banks and actions of commercial banks. This complexity and multiple causality challenge the existence of a simple, stable, long-run direct relation between prices and money. Keynes smacks QTM orthodoxy when saying:

> But this *long run* [proportionality between money and prices] is a mislead-ing guide to current affairs. *In the long run we are all dead.* Economists set themselves too easy, too useless a task if in tempestuous seasons they can tell us that when the storm is long past the ocean is flat again.
>
> (TMR, p. 80)

This phrase caught people's imagination and is one of his most famous state-ments. In terms of policy, Keynes proposes not only the stabilisation of the price level in the long run but also moderation of price fluctuations in the short run through deliberate, prudent and indirect actions by the central banks affecting the stock of money in circulation (n) and the cash ratio held by the banks (r). Furthermore, monetary authorities can influence, in an indirect way, the preference for cash and cheques by the public and business. JMK leans in favour of a monetary policy of active management of n and the bank rate to affect r and counterbalance potential changes in k and k′ all aiming to reduce fluctuations in p (price level).

Monetary authorities may lose control of n in at least two cases: firstly, un-der conditions of very high inflation as the public escapes away from the use or holding of money to avoid being affected by the inflation tax, and secondly, in the case of the operation of the unregulated gold standard in which the creation or reduction of the money supply follows the inflows and outflows of gold. In this case, the central banks would abstain from "sterilising" (through open-market operations) the flows of metallic in and out of the country. For Keynes, cyclical fluctuations in the money market and the economy-wide are driven more by changes in k and k′ (demand for money) rather than by changes in n and r (supply of money and credit). The Keynes proposal was for a reasonably *accommodative* monetary policy aimed at the stabilisation of the price level and smoothing the business cycle. He was highly scepti-cal of the wisdom and practical feasibility of adopting rigid policy rules that fix the stock of money (or its rate of change) irrespective of the behaviour of the demand for money and its determinants (habits, social and business norms and interest rates). It is safe to assume that he would have disagreed with Milton Friedman's rule of fixed money growth. This is a rule that could induce economic upswings and downswings of economic activity (booms and recessions) if it is not accommodating to changes in the demand for money. In contrast, a monetary policy that is wisely accommodative can avoid undue fluctuations in real economic activity that cause economic hardship (unem-ployment) and disappointment in expectations.

The Theory of Purchasing Power Parity

The analysis of Chapter 3 of the TMR continues with the determination of the exchange rate (the purchasing power of the local currency in terms of a foreign currency). In a world of inconvertible currencies, the doctrine of the Purchasing Power Parity, associated with David Ricardo and Gustav Cassel, states that:

i The *internal* purchasing power of an inconvertible currency (in terms of domestic goods) is associated with the monetary and credit policy of central banks and the predictions of the quantity theory of money.

ii The *external* purchasing power of money in terms of foreign goods is the exchange rate between the home and foreign currency adjusted by the foreign currency purchasing power in its own country.

iii In equilibrium, the external and internal purchasing power of a currency must be equal (adjusting for transport costs and taxes on international trade). Otherwise, there will be an incentive for arbitrage in the movement of goods through international trade due to significant discrepancies in prices between countries (importing goods from cheaper countries and exporting to countries with higher prices). From conditions (i), (ii) and (iii), it follows that:

$$e = P/P^*$$
(3.2)

This relation says that the exchange rate (units of local currency per one unit of foreign currency) is equal to the ratio of the domestic price level, P, and the foreign price level, P^*, or in other words as the ratio between the internal purchasing power of each currency in its own country. In the world of the classic gold standard, the exchange rate was the ratio of gold units per unit of local and foreign currency.

It must be noted that *observed* exchange rates may *differ* from the ratios between domestic and foreign price levels and be more fluctuating than the ratio in the price levels of countries. Another difficulty that the doctrine of Purchasing Power Parity faces is how to treat the fact that there are goods that do not enter foreign trade and thus are not shipped internationally. This is the case for example of services like haircuts and other "home goods" such as land and houses that are internationally immobile although can be acquired by foreigners. However, a degree of substitution between international trade and home goods does exist exerting a convergence between local and foreign goods.

Markets for foreign exchange can be organised on a "spot basis" in which the delivery of foreign currency is immediate with cash/cheques delivered instantaneously to the seller or buyer of foreign exchange or can be organised on a "forward basis" in which units of foreign exchange are to be delivered at a future date according to a suitable contract in which the price of the transaction is *set in advance*. Nonetheless, the actual payment is made in the future (a part of the contract may be required to be paid in advance). Forward exchange markets tend to reduce the risk of exchange rate fluctuations affecting a trade transaction or a foreign debt payment. Therefore, they are expected to contribute to stabilise international trade by reducing the uncertainty of variability in the value of the exchange rate facing traders in the international marketplace during the duration of the contract. In practice, however, forward markets may not be very deep and liquid due to the existence of transaction costs that reduce the accessibility to this market by international traders, banks and debt holders.

Objectives of Monetary Policy

Chapter 4 of the TMR discusses what should be the main aim of monetary policy in the concrete historical realities of post-war Europe, featuring inflation, instability and the end of the gold standard.

Three forms of stabilisation are highlighted:

1 The dilemma between devaluation and deflation in fixing exchange parities either to the dollar, other currencies or gold.
2 The stabilisation of the domestic value of the currency (internal price level) versus the stabilisation of the external value of the currency (exchange rate stabilisation).
3 The restoration of the gold standard

In the choice between devaluation and deflation, the implicit criteria are how to move the current (observed) exchange rate to an equilibrium exchange rate in countries that have experienced different rates of inflation. The choice is between adjusting the exchange rate or adjusting the domestic price level. This simply follows the doctrine (equation) of purchasing power parity. The route of the *devaluation* implies, of course, depreciating the local currency to close the gap between domestic and international prices. Specifically, devaluing the currency implies lowering the number of units of foreign currency required to acquire one unit of local currency, or – what is the same – giving more units of local currency per unit of foreign currency. The other alternative is *deflating* (reducing) domestic prices by compressing wages to allow a restoration of purchasing power parity. At the time the *Tract* was written, the discussion in economic and financial circles was on the convenience or not of restoring countries' parities to gold at pre-war 1913 levels as it was proposed by the financial orthodoxy on grounds of national pride and the prestige of having a stronger national currency. Keynes' preference, however, was for the *devaluation* of the national currency. The alternative of deflation was bound to reduce employment and production forcing a recessive adjustment to get certain desired parity. It was clearly a costly option in terms of sacrifice of employment, production and living standards.

Regarding the stabilisation of the price level versus the stabilisation of foreign exchange, it is important to recognise that the stabilisation of both magnitudes at the same time is not possible by the relation of purchasing power parity stated above. In fact, if external inflation is higher than internal inflation, an adjustment of the exchange rate is required for internal prices to remain stable. If the exchange rate is not adjusted, external inflation will be reflected in domestic inflation. By simple inspection, it is apparent that *both* P and e cannot be held constant if PPP is to hold.

In the era of the classic gold standard, exchange rate stability was preferred, and therefore, e was maintained fixed relative to gold. Reasonable internal price stability followed to the extent of external inflation and the price of gold was reasonably stable. This was not always the case, for example, after the massive discoveries of gold in Australia, California and South Africa that led to an increase in the international supply of gold and the concomitant rise in the supply of domestic money with internal inflationary consequences for the countries engaged in the gold standard.

After WWI, in the transition to a new international monetary system, possibly to a reconstructed gold standard, the stabilisation of the exchange rate was not an easy task as the pre-1914 mechanism of the gold anchor was not around. Using the US dollar as a new international standard was a possibility but Europe did not want to depend too much on the decisions of the American Federal Reserve Bank, created only in 1913. In these conditions, Keynes' proposition was to orient monetary policy to stabilise the price level.

The restoration of the gold standard in the conditions of the fragile settlement after World War I and the rise of the United States as a main hegemonic country were seen with scepticism by JMK. The world of international monetary cooperation of the last decades of the classic gold standard was largely gone. Moreover, wage and price flexibility were reduced after WWI with the emerging activism of labour unions and the development of oligopolistic market structures. The gold standard needed downward wage and price flexibility to operate, and this was politically more difficult to attain in the 1920s than in the pre-1914 era. Keynes recognised the benefits in terms of stability and predictability of the gold standard of the 19th century, but he was also aware that the conditions that allowed for the functioning of the system were very unlikely to replicate in the foreseeable future, given the new realities of the 1920s. In addition, JMK saw countries that could afford it, to hoard gold, delinking the accumulation of the metal from its monetary uses. The value of gold was no longer determined by the chances of nature and decisions of several independent governments and their central banks. Now the value of gold will depend on the decisions of three or four most powerful central banks. A possible shortage of gold was also noted by some observers.

A demonetisation of gold in the context of an increasingly powerful US dollar with the augmented influence of the US Federal Reserve on the value of gold created the problem of what was to be a reliable standard of value of the dollar. In a world of "managed currencies", the stability of currencies will depend on the actions and judgements of finance ministers and state banks whose soundness and wise behaviour were not always guaranteed. Keynes was aware that there were little good options for a stable international monetary system in the environment of the 1920s. He opposed a restoration of the gold standard on pre-war lines while at the same time remained concerned on the ability of a managed gold standard – under strong US influence and highly dependent on the decisions of the American central bank – to guarantee stability, predictability and confidence worldwide. His preference was for a mixed system of dollar standard and sterling standard with close coordination between the American Fed and the Bank of England. Countries would hold gold but supplemented by holding of dollar reserves and sterling reserves.

Positive Suggestions for the Future Regulation of Money

Coming back to the level of the national economy, JMK shifts to what should be the criteria for stabilisation of the internal value of the currency. In this connection, he proposes a dual policy of (i) regulating the supply of currency and credit oriented to stabilise the internal price level and (ii) a policy of regulation of the supply of foreign exchange oriented to stabilise the foreign exchange market.

The underlying theory is that the price level is determined by the supply of credit by the banking system and the money supply. The stock of credit in a fractional banking system depends on the volume of deposits received from the public by the banks and the proportion of those deposits held in cash (currency notes and coins) at the central bank (Bank of England) by commercial banks. A rule of thumb is that a proportion of around 10 percent of the deposits are held in cash. So, 9 out of 10 pounds deposited in the banks could be potentially subject to credit expansion.

The amount of liquidity circulating in the economy will depend on the assets that are acquired by the central bank (an expansion of assets in the balance sheet) and that pay through the issuance of money which corresponds to an increase in its liabilities.

The following three main purchases are often made by central banks:

1   Treasury Bills (helping to finance the national treasury)
2   Advances to commercial banks in exchange for commercial paper (rediscount operations)
3   Purchases of gold

Following equation (3.1) above –Keynes' formulation of the quantity theory of money –, the price level depends on the stock of currency in circulation (notes and cheques) and the reserve ratios held in cash by commercial banks. The stock of credit is lower the higher the proportion of deposits held in cash as less resources are available to make new credit and finance other investments carried out by the banks.

Fiscal policy and the ways fiscal spending is financed also affect liquidity. For example, if the treasury sells bonds that are acquired by the central bank, this institution creates a monetary base that is spent by the government. Thus, in this framework, both fiscal policy and monetary policy parameters and banking policy affect the price level. For stabilising prices, certain restrictions are placed on the behaviour of the central bank (monetary policy), the treasury (fiscal policy) and the commercial banks (credit policy). Keynes does a job in the TMR of explaining the operation of these credit-money mechanisms that, given their complexity, cannot be expected to be always clear to the public, authorities and academics.

As the gold standard is no longer in operation, "gold is immobilised". In contrast with the world up to 1913, the Bank of England neither sells or buys gold for monetary purposes in the first half of the 1920s. At the same time, the foreign exchanges are unregulated and freely fluctuating with the price of foreign currency in local currency being determined by the interplay of supply and demand for sterling, dollar and other international currencies. This is in obvious contrast with the policy of fixing the exchange rate in terms of gold utilised during the regime of the gold standard in which monetary authorities are willing to buy or sell unlimited amounts of gold at a set parity between the local currency and gold. In a "pure (unregulated)" gold standard system, the money supply becomes endogenously determined and fluctuates according to the purchases and sales of gold. In a system of freely floating exchange rates, the supply of money and the supply of credit becomes more autonomous and depends on the central bank policy of buying assets and the level of the discount rate. For JMK, the primary objective must be the stabilisation of prices in sterling followed by the stabilisation of the sterling-dollar exchange rate in cooperation with the American Federal Reserve Bank in the stabilisation of dollar prices to avoid fluctuations in the exchange rate between two currencies. Irving Fisher also gave priority to the stabilisation prices in dollars (internal price level) and termed this policy a "compensated dollar". He proposed a policy of automatic adjustment of the money supply to a certain price index. Keynes doubted "the practicality of a system so cut and dry". Among the reasons for his scepticism is the lag in the data of prices that adjust more delayed; in addition, what matters is future prices rather than past prices, argued JMK.

Keynes advocated for a regulation of the price of gold in sterling, say having a buying and selling price of gold to stabilise the exchanges but refrained from advocating the fixing or "pegging" the sterling price of gold. In this case, the gold rate along with the bank rate would be the two instruments to regulate credit and foreign exchanges in the conduct of monetary policy.

Summary

The *Tract* aims at promoting "monetary reform", say criteria – but not rigid rules – for the conduct of monetary policy in a world no longer attached to the gold standard. He urged us to learn from the experience of this monetary system, including limitations, before 1913. The chief aim of monetary policy, according to JMK, must be the stabilisation of the purchasing power of money, a far from simple task. This may entail stabilising its internal value or its external value, which are not necessarily identical criteria. In addition, simple rules such as stabilising the supply of money may be counterproductive if the demand for money is unstable, warned Keynes. These observations have obvious relevance for nowadays tasks of central banks.

The TMR offers an insightful look at the effects of unanticipated inflation and identifies winners and losers from price increases, identifies the pros and cons involved in the use of the inflation tax, identifies the purchasing power doctrine of exchange rate determination and offers criteria for conducting monetary policy.

The *Tract* underscores the inertia in the contract structure of the economy (wages, house rents, financial contracts) and is aware of the limited institutional adaptation to inflation of the 1910s and 1920s in Europe. The "rentier class" is adversely affected by inflation but traders and producers, merchants, manufacturers and agriculturists finance their activities with debt will benefit. Conversely, deflation affects producers but benefits the rentiers. These are redistributive effects. At the same time, inflation penalises savings, investment and growth on account of uncertainty effects. On the contrary, deflation, according to Keynes, could be worse and bring about recession harming employment creation. The Tract, although not arguing in favour of a policy of *constant* prices, shows that very high inflation can have destructive effects on the economic system by reducing the use of money by the public as monetary balances become heavily taxed in hyperinflation.

Rampant inflation creates very high uncertainty and penalises capital formation, leading to the collapse of growth as inflation gets out of hand. In the TMR, the cases of "hyperinflation" – the term, however, does not appear in the book – are Germany, Austria and Russia in the early 1920s. Other, more contemporaneous, episodes of extreme inflation in Greece in 1941–1945, Yugoslavia in 1990–1993, Peru in 1988–1990, Nicaragua in 1986–1991 and Venezuela in 2017–2018 for which the logic of the inflation tax and calculation of the dynamics of its collection and the shift away from money developed in the *Tract* can be relevant to understand more contemporaneous episodes of extreme inflation.[2]

The book offers new vistas underscoring the role played by changes in the demand for money and the importance of the preference for cash by the public, firms and banks in the determination of the price level. Causality shifts from the supply side to the demand side of the money market in contrast with the standard orthodox reading of the QTM. In addition, it shows the central bank's control of base money and the discount rate as influencing the cash-deposits ratio of the banking system, a key parameter that affects the ability to create credit and affect the price level. So, it provides a mixed story of money (a liability) and credit (asset) interacting in their influence on the price level and the business cycle.

In the *Tract,* monetary policy must stabilise the price level but no fixed money supply rules a la Milton Friedman proposed. On the contrary, the supply of money must be flexible and adjust to changes in demand for money (changes in velocity).

In a world no longer ruled by the gold standard, policymakers must be aware of the various dilemmas present in the process of stabilising the value of money: should it be the internal value of money (in terms of commodities or consumption goods in the national economy) or should it be a stabilisation in terms of foreign goods and the exchange rate? The classic gold standard was oriented to the stabilisation of the value of money in terms of a *commodity* such as gold. Prices did experience fluctuations due to the discoveries of new gold, and central banks, particularly between 1890 and 1913, had to struggle with the need to keep the supply of money reasonably stable due to the buying and selling of gold.

After the abandonment of the gold, monetary authorities were left without the gold anchor. The stabilisation of domestic prices had to be undertaken by central banks with help from the ministries of finance. After the monetary edifice of the gold standard, supposedly dominated by rules, crumbled, monetary policy started to depend to a large degree on the actions, judgements and fallibilities of central bank officials and treasury officers. The trust on monetary authorities deteriorated when the inflation tax was actively used to finance very large fiscal deficits.

Keynes proposed the use of the discount rate, the buying and selling of assets, including treasury bills, to regulate liquidity in the economy and stabilise the price level. These issues have been at the core of the design and practice of stabilisation policy and the sustainability in public finances and the balance payments in different countries in different critical junctures: after WWII, in the inflationary 1970s in advanced economies, in the 1970s and 1980s in Latin America, Turkey, the Philippines in the 1980s, in post-socialist countries that started their transition to market economies in the 1990s and so on.

Notes

1 Fetter (1977).
2 Solimano (2020).

4 *A Treatise on Money.* Wicksell, Bulls and Bears

Introduction

This chapter is devoted to the analysis of *A Treatise on Money* (TM). The *Treatise* started to be written in 1924 and was published in 1930 in two volumes that reached a total of around 760 pages (the TMR was only 205 pages long). The TM followed the *Tract* published in 1923 and preceded *The General Theory of Employment, Interest and Money* published in 1936. The book appeared after the stock market crash of 1929 in the United States that triggered a protracted global economic slump – the great depression – affecting Great Britain, the United States, Central Europe and regions of the periphery of the world economy. It was written at a time when the British economy reflected the decline of the British empire: since the early 1920s and until the end of the decade, unemployment remained at around 10 percent, and the industrial structure was rigid. These trends were aggravated following the restoration of the pre-World War parity between the British pound and gold in 1925.

However, the *Treatise* was more theoretical than a policy-oriented book which was the case of the *Tract*. An important analytical motivation of Keynes was to revise the existing theory of money, largely dominated by the quantity theory, and propose a new framework that could be consistent with the historical record and current facts of the 1920s. The TM was inspired by Wicksell and had the influence of the QTM.

The *Treatise* explores critical issues in the definition of money and its purchasing power in terms of consumption goods (commodities), wholesale prices and the price of output (GDP deflator) and foreign goods. Volume I explores relevant connections between central bank policy, the banking system, investment, savings, profits and prices. Of special interest for Keynes was getting a better understanding of the dynamics of prices out of equilibrium as it affects "the value of money". The QTM was focused on a long-run equilibrium, but JMK wanted a theory for the transition between long runs. A concern of the book is the transmission mechanism from money to the real side of the economy based on the interest rate (the "bank-rate") and the influence of the

DOI: 10.4324/9781003480785-4

banking system in the creation of liquidity and provision of credit with effects on investment, savings, interest rates and prices. In addition, the *Treatise,* in line with the *Tract,* but unlike the *General Theory* that is largely "a closed economy" book, deals with an economy that is internationally integrated with capital markets and therefore not only trade flows but also financial flows matter for the determination of overall macroeconomic equilibrium. In this line, JMK devoted substantial space to examine issues of internal equilibrium and external monetary equilibrium and the ensuing dilemmas to policymakers. The internal equilibrium is given by the equality between savings and investment and external equilibrium stems from the interaction between the current account of the balance of payments (movements of goods and services and factor payments) and the capital account (movements of foreign direct investment and foreign lending) with inflows and outflows of gold settling the imbalances of external payments.

The *Treatise* is influenced, at a conceptual level, by, at least, four different strands of thought:

i   Dennis H. Robertson's book *Banking Policy and the Price Level* (Robertson, 1926) is a book that Keynes himself collaborated directly with Robertson in different stages of its preparation. A complex issue at the time was the definition of savings. Robertson used the concept of "hoarding", while referring to the compression of consumption (savings) as "lacking" (automatic or induced). The controversy on the meaning of savings would continue for a few years.[1]

ii Another influence is Irving Fisher's *The Purchasing Power of Money: Its Determination in Relation to Credit, Interest and Crises* (Fisher, 1911) reflected in the early chapters of Book I that focus on the use of alternative price indices to calculate the purchasing power of money. Fisher's theories are also used in the development of the "Fundamental Equations for the Value of Money" in equilibrium. Keynes stresses that there is a plurality of price levels, and the stabilisation in the value of money must be defined in terms of certain price indices.[2]

iii The *Treatise* follows the tradition of Knut Wicksell's of the Stockholm School of Economics. Particularly important is the influence of Wicksell's *Interest and Prices: A Study of the Causes Regulating the Value of Money* (Wicksell, 1911 [1936]), which investigates a mechanism of transmission from money to prices that goes beyond the mathematical identity of the quantitative theory of money and the Walras law (an excess supply of money creates an excess demand in the goods market). Wicksell presents a formulation of the *market for loanable funds* with the supply of funds originating in the savings capacity of individuals and the demand for loanable funds coming from the demand for investment by enterprises. When there is an excess of investment over savings, there is credit creation with monetary consequences. Wicksell introduces the distinction between the *market interest rate* influenced by bank credit and the money supply and the *natural interest rate* equivalent to the marginal productivity of capital and savings and investment equilibrium. The *Treatise* replaces the loanable funds market for the savings-investment (in)balance but keeps the distinction between the market interest rate and the natural interest rate. The *Treatise* also devotes substantial space to examine the working of the commercial banking system and its interaction with central banks in the creation of money and how this affects credit cycles and the behaviour of investment and savings.

iv The TM adopts an investment-led growth perspective in which investment, animal spirits and a drive for action by entrepreneurs boost economic expansion. For Keynes, it is investment not savings that brings about economic stimulus and prosperity. Savings plays an accommodating role in the demand for investment but thrift does not *initiate* a process of growth. In this perspective, Keynes follows, without necessarily admitting fully, the views of Marx and Schumpeter on the role of the entrepreneur (bourgeois) in fostering economic change and development through the adoption for productive purposes of new technologies and innovations. Volume II elaborates on the stimulus for capital accumulation coming from discoveries of valuable natural resources such as the arrival of gold and silver to Spain after the discovery of America that created waves of optimism in the "investment community". The focus of JMK on the importance of investment contrasts with his "savings pessimism", in the sense that the progress of capitalism rarely is associated with thrift, frugality and savings as causal factors. His parable of the *savings paradox* in the island leading to a zero-output equilibrium conveys the idea that an increase in savings can be downright contractive, reducing incomes and employment. His view was that first comes an autonomous increase in investment followed by a passive adjustment in savings. This story will play a central role in the *General Theory*. Moreover, JMK believed in a low-interest rate elasticity of savings.

v In addition, the *Treatise* presents an implicit mechanism of "forced savings" following a forced compression in consumption associated with increases in the price level that reduce the purchasing power of income. This was to be developed later more fully by Nicholas Kaldor and the "Post-Keynesian"-Cambridge (UK) School using the Ricardian insight that capitalists have a higher propensity to save than workers. An increase in the price level creates windfall profits that are mostly saved. At the same time, the price rise depresses real wages compressing overall consumption as workers have a higher propensity to consume than capital owners. Profit inflation is a main theme in the *Treatise,* and since it originated in an imbalance between savings and investment, there is an endogenous mechanism that closes the gap between the two variables through an increase in savings and an implicit redistributive effect between labour and capital (the redistributive effect is *not* worked out explicitly by Keynes).

An important theoretical contribution of the *Treatise* derives from a "fundamental set of price equations" obtained using income, output and expenditure identities. This focus on expenditure-income identities is maintained in the *General Theory*. In turn, the quantity equation identity focuses on the supply of money and the demand for money although it can be also identified as an equality between total nominal spending and the total nominal value of output. Both formulations: the QTM and TM's fundamental equations are equivalent in the long-run equilibrium under the assumptions of wage and price flexibility and market interest rates equalising the natural rate. The *Treatise*'s formulation of disequilibrium positions through the fundamental equations adds to the analysis of several mechanisms that are really not considered in the quantity theory such as profit disequilibrium and forced savings. Issues of methodology in macroeconomics, the treatment of time, the meaning of equilibrium and convergence are taken up at the end of this chapter.

An underlying assumption of the *Treatise* is that economies converge to a full employment equilibrium, admitting transitory variations of output and employment around that norm along the lines of business cycle theories. In the TM, Keynes was especially interested in explaining fluctuations in the general price level echoing the focus of the quantity theory of money ($MV = PO$).[3] Another main concern of the *Treatise* – developed more fully in the *General Theory* – is to explain how a monetary economy is different from a "real-exchange economy" in which money is only a device to economise the often-significant transaction costs of a barter economy in which there is a need for double coincidence of goods to materialise transactions and can affect the real side of the economy (production and employment). In the world of quantity theory, money is not intended to affect real transactions or the motives and decisions of the parties engaged in those transactions. In that sense, money is considered *neutral*. Keynes in the *Treatise* still considers neutrality as a valid long-run result but in disequilibrium positions – chiefly due to discrepancies between savings and investment – money ceases to be neutral.

A Tour of the *Treatise*

A Treatise on Money is composed of two volumes: Volume I devoted to "The Pure Theory of Money" (mainly theoretical), and Volume II focused on "The Applied Theory of Money" which is more empirical, applied and historical.

Volume I. The Pure Theory of Money

Chapter 1 (Book I) analyses the origins and evolution of state money and bank money (coins and notes) offering typologies that include commodity standards, fiat money, representative money and managed money. Chapters 2 and 3 offer a discussion of bank money and the role of different types of deposits (income, business, savings) in creating bank money. JMK alerts of the potential instabilities that are present in this process through bank lending. Book II, including Chapters 4–8, examines "the value of money" and its purchasing power in terms of bundles of goods. The *price of money* is the inverse of the price level of goods (and not the interest rate).

The reader is guided through various measurements of the purchasing power of money in terms of consumption goods, earning standards and working-class Index Numbers.

Book III represents the analytical core of the book. It formulates "The Fundamental Equations of Money" (Chapters 9–14) starting with basic definitions of income, profits, savings and investment. Income is viewed both from the cost side as payments to the factors of production (wages, a normal remuneration to entrepreneurs) as well as its uses for consumption and investment. At the same time, there is a separate category of (excess) profits – or just profits – to entrepreneurs that are equal to the difference between incomes and the cost of production. Profits exist when investment is greater than savings; conversely, losses (negative profits) are the surplus of savings over investment. Profits are *not* considered as an income category; only the normal remuneration of entrepreneurs is included.

The use of income is equal to consumption plus investment. In equilibrium, savings (adjusted by windfall profits) is equal to investment. Keynes defines savings as income minus consumption. Investment, in turn, represents an "addition to national wealth" and can be separated into fixed capital investment (long-lived productive assets), working capital (goods-in-process), and inputs and liquid capital (unsold production or inventories).

In the aggregate, the motives of those agents who save are not necessarily the same motives of those who invest. Therefore, the two variables may differ as planned or intended magnitudes (ex-ante), although ex-post they must be equal. A discrepancy between intended savings and planned investment has important implications for macro equilibrium and the relevant adjustment variable in the macro system. In the *Tract* and the *Treatise,* the critical adjustment variable to bring equality between planned investment and intended savings is the *price level,* while in the *General Theory,* it is the *level of output and employment.* Price versus quantity adjustment is a main theme in the analysis of Keynes's macroeconomics, and which variable adjusts can vary through its different books (see Patinkin, 1965, 1982).

In the *Treatise,* JMK distinguishes between "available output", say output available for consumption and "non-available output". The latter corresponds to investment. Definitions also include the "foreign balance" and its current account and capital account components.

The analysis starts with the quantity equation (Chapter 10):

$$\text{Money} \times \text{Velocity} = \text{Prices} \times \text{Output} \qquad (4.1)$$

or

$$MV = PO \qquad (4.1')$$

The QTM equation presents at least two features that render macro analysis potentially ambiguous (Vol I, Book III Chapter 10, p. 133):

a $MV = PO$ is compatible with various directions of causality among money and prices (from M to P or from P to M). In addition, the equation is not explicit on the dynamics of the price level (and output) in the transition moving from one equilibrium position to another.

The quantity equation does not apply to a purchasing power concept (bundle of consumption of goods) or a labour standard (number of hours worked) that provides a meaningful valuation of money.

The Fundamental Equations of the TM (Price Levels)

The two fundamental equations are the price level of consumption goods, Pc, and the price level of total output, P. For Keynes, the price level of consumption goods represents the genuine purchasing power of money.

Definitions start from earnings, E (= money income), and its distribution between consumption (C) and savings (S), say $E = C + S$. In turn, output (O) is the sum of consumption (C) and investment (I), say $O = C + I$.

Using the identity Consumption = Earnings − Savings and the definitions of output and earnings, Keynes arrives to a price level of consumption goods, Pc[4]:

$$Pc = E/O + (I - S)/Qc \qquad (4.2)$$

where Qc is the quantity of consumption goods.

Let W be the rate of earnings (factor payments) per unit of effort and e be the coefficient of efficiency, we get:

$$Pc = W/e + (I - S)/Qc \qquad (4.2')$$

Then, prices are the sum of two components:

Price = cost of production/factor earnings (in efficiency units) + imbalance between investment and savings.

Alternatively:

Price = factor earnings (in efficiency units) + profit rate

The price equation is a decomposition of the unitary cost of production (wages, inputs, the normal remuneration of entrepreneurs) and excess profits of output produced. Also, remember that factor earnings are also equivalent to money income. *Excess Profits arise in a macro disequilibrium position, say when investment exceeds savings.* In a stationary equilibrium, profit will disappear, and prices will be stable (Marshallian long-run equilibrium).

The second fundamental equation for the *price level of output* as a whole, P, is:

$$P = E/O + (I - S)/O \tag{4.3}$$

or

$$P = W/e + (I - S)/O \tag{4.4}$$

Again, the second fundamental equation for the price of the whole output is a function of both the costs of production (in efficiency terms) and the imbalance between investment and savings.

If I > S, then P > E/O and (abnormal) profits are created. This encourages investment, increasing the demand for factors of production and pushing up their earnings, E, until a new equilibrium is restored. Conversely if S > I, then P < E/O with firms experiencing losses (negative profits) that push down factor remunerations. An equilibrium without abnormal profits is achieved only when I = S and then P = E/O.

For the dynamics, an equation for the rate of change of prices, dP/dt, can be defined as a function F[.] of the investment-savings imbalance, say:

$$dP/dt = F\left[(I - S)/O\right]$$

The price level will be stable, dP = 0, when F(0) = 0, or I = S. In other words, when savings=investment.

How can we reconcile the quantity of money equation (4.1) in which the price of output is a function of the money supply and the velocity of circulation (output is constant at full employment) with a price equation (in terms of consumption goods or total output) obtained from basic identities between incomes (earnings), output and expenditure (national accounts relationships)?

If we replace equation (4.1) MV = PO in the fundamental equation for the price level of total output (4.3) P = E/O + (I − S)/O and noting that E = MV, we get:

$$P = MV/O + I - S/O \tag{4.5}$$

By the quantity equation, $MV/O = P$.

Then (4.5) and (4.1) will be equal only if $I = S$.

Keynes lists the conditions of macro equilibrium for a reconciliation between the quantity theory and his fundamental equations. In his own words:

> … in equilibrium when the factors of production are fully employed, when the public is neither bullish nor bearish of securities and is maintaining in the form of saving-deposits, neither more nor less than the "normal" proportion of its total wealth, and when the volume of savings is equal both the cost and value of new investment—there is a unique relationship between the quantity of money and the price level of consumption goods and of output as a whole, of such character that if the quantity of money were double the price level would double also.
>
> But this simple and direct quantitative relationship is a phenomenon only of equilibrium as defined above. If the volume of savings becomes unequal to the cost of new investment, or if the public disposition towards securities, even for good reasons, in the bullish or bearish directions, then the fundamental price-levels can depart from their equilibrium values without any change having occurred in the quantity of money or the velocity of circulation.
>
> (Vol. I, Book III, chapter 10, p. 147)

This is an important analytical result, showing that money neutrality – money growth equal to the rate of change in the price level – is valid only if the following three conditions are met:

1 There are no imbalances in the goods market or, what is the same, savings is equal to investment.
2 The securities market is in equilibrium.
3 Output is at full employment.

However, money neutrality breaks down in *disequilibrium positions*. In this case, the second term of equation (4.5) represents a disequilibrium factor (the discrepancy of investment to savings). Keynes, in the TM, was particularly interested in out-of-equilibrium trajectories.

Then in Chapter 11, the conditions of economic equilibrium are developed. It starts with the condition that in equilibrium, profits must be zero as:

Profits = Value of output – Cost of production = Value of investment – Savings.

Therefore, in equilibrium:

Investment = Savings (zero profits conditions)

Note, however, that if abnormal profits were included in the definition of income (or earnings/costs of production), they would be part of savings and no imbalance between investment and savings would arise.

Connections with the Banking System

The banking system plays an important role in the analysis of the *Treatise* on account of its dual role of receiving saving deposits from the public and firms that can be loaned to enterprises and households and invested in securities (stocks and bonds). Banks play two roles: (a) as financial intermediaries or *credit-making entities* pooling deposits from the public and channelling them into the supply of loans to enterprises and households and (b) as providers of *liquidity* through cash deposits (checking accounts).

Keynes stresses that bank money is a substitute for state money (coins and notes issued by a central bank). Banks act as a clearing house transferring payments forward and backward to different customers. Monetary analysis (liquidity) and credit analysis (financial intermediation) are both relevant.

Bank credit can finance working capital needs such as paying wages, buying inputs and holding in-process goods. Loans also can finance long-term investment in long-lived assets such as building, houses, infrastructure and so on which is more relevant to the long-term interest rate. Short- and long-term interest rates, the so-called term structure of interest rates, may differ depending on the use of credit by customers (working capital versus long-term investment projects).

The operation of bank money can be viewed as the lifeblood of an economic system with a critical role played by the banking system in helping to ensure the attainment of macroeconomic equilibrium.

In Keynes terms:

> Thus the conditions for the equilibrium of the purchasing power of money requires that the Banking System should so regulate its rate of lending that the value of Investment is equal to Savings; for otherwise entrepreneurs will, under the influence of positive or negative profits, be both willing in themselves and at the same time influenced by the abundance or scarcity of bank-credit to their disposal to increase or diminish, as the case may be, the average remuneration they offer to the factors of production.
>
> (Vol. I, Book III, chapter 11, p. 152)

This remark is based on the "fundamental equations". The price level is *in equilibrium* – absence of either inflationary or deflationary pressures – when there are no abnormal profits and savings = investment.

The *Treatise* also describes adjustments in the level of output and employment "between production periods" although the centrality of this mechanism will be only stressed, later, in the *General Theory*.

In disequilibrium positions, a key role is played by bank credit that allows investment to exceed savings, leading to an increase in the price level (assuming constant, in a first round, the cost of production). However, the imbalance between saving and investment will generate a second round of disequilibrium in which profits (or losses) will push up (or down) factor remunerations that must be curbed in some way by the banking system.

The Bank Rate

The *Treatise* was looking for a variable to transmit changes in the supply of money (and other monetary disturbances) on investment and savings. The presumption is that the demand for investment is more sensitive to interest rate changes than the supply of savings. In turn, investment, critically affected by expectations, is generally more volatile than savings, which fluctuate more smoothly.

Then, an increase in the interest rate reduces investment and (moderately) increases savings, correcting the initial excess of investment over savings and bringing down the price level.

The *Treatise* works with two sets of interest rates: (a) the natural rate of interest and the market interest rate (following Wicksell's *Interest and Prices*) and (b) short-term and long-run interest rates. The market and natural interest rates will be equal when there is no imbalance between investment and savings, and the second term of the fundamental equation is equal to zero.

JMK, always fond of making different classifications in his writings, labels an increase in prices due to adjustment in the first component of the fundamental equation (4.2) as *income inflation* (or deflation). An increase in prices due to a change in the second component of (4.2), say the imbalance between savings and investment, corresponds to *profit inflation* (or deflation).

Income inflation would be equivalent to what we ascribe as "cost-push inflation", say increases in wages and the domestic cost of imported inputs, while Profit Inflation would be equivalent to "excess demand inflation" or overheating in the goods market (in more modern usage). In the TM, this corresponds to "commodity inflation".

Summing up, the three conditions of long-run macroeconomic equilibrium are as follows:

1 Investment = savings
2 Market interest rate = natural interest rate
3 Stability of the price level

Chapters 13 and 37 of the TM elaborate in more detail on how the interest rates – the "bank rate" – work out their way through credit, savings, investment and prices. The money interest rate is determined in the loanable funds market (depending on the supply and demand for money and credit), and the natural rate of interest makes savings equal to investment. The book also stresses the relevance of the expected profitability of investment and works out the open economy modification of the fundamental price equation to allow for foreign savings.

Chapter 13 (Vol. I, Book III) on "The 'Modus Operandi' of the Bank rate" explores the following question: how an adjustment in the rate of interest the central bank charges to commercial banks for discounting documents (advance liquidity) affects the price level (and the international balance of payments)? The following three mechanisms are possible:

1 By making credit more expensive, commercial banks diminish their volume of loans, thereby reducing the stock of bank money (or its rate of creation) and reducing the price level according to the predictions of the quantity equation.
2 A second interpretation, for an open economy, referred to by JMK as "the view of practical bankers", is that a rise in the bank rate is oriented to protect (increase) the gold reserves by attracting capital inflows (foreign lending) from abroad. In other words, interest rate policy is oriented to maintaining *external balance* (in the international balance of payments) rather than *internal balance* (savings = investment). Conflicts between internal and external balance may arise.
3 A third mechanism is to increase the bank rate to reduce an imbalance between investment and savings which is required to ensure price stability.[5]

The third mechanism, preferred by JMK, has a close resemblance to the interest theory of Knut Wicksell who defined the interest rate that is neutral as one that does not exert any upward or downward pressure on the price level; therefore, for the market interest rate to eliminate any discrepancy between investment and savings, it must coincide with the neutral/natural interest rate.

If the market interest rate is *below* the natural rate, there will be an excess of investment over savings provoking an upward pressure on prices (inflationary pressure). Conversely, if the market interest rate is *above* the natural rate, that situation will exert deflationary pressure on prices. Only when the natural rate of interest = the market interest rate, investment = savings, and prices are stable.[6]

The story can be summarised as follows:

a The central bank discount rate affects the money interest rate or "bank rate" which is the effective interest rate prevailing in the market for loans.
b An equilibrium of price stability will be reached when the money interest rate is equal to the natural interest rate.

JMK Reassessment of the Quantity Theory (QT)

In Chapter 14 (Volume I), Keynes returns to the theme of the quantity theory of money, distinguishing among three formulations:

1   The *real balances formulation*: This representation is adopted in the *Tract on Monetary Reform* in which real balances are held to *finance consumption expenditures*.
2   The *Cambridge formulation*: This is associated with Marshall and Pigou in which the demand for money is a function of either the *level of real income* or the "general resources" of the economy.
3   *Irving Fisher*'s formulation: In his book *The Purchasing Power of Money*, he linked monetary balances to the *volume of transactions* in the economy.

JMK notes that the QTM framework is not particularly well suited to study changes in the "value of money", among other reasons, because the different formulations of the QTM imply distinct price levels. They can be closer to a monetary standard (fitting each relevant formulation) rather than a genuine index of the purchasing power of money in terms of consumption goods. Other complexities affecting the quantity theory of money refer to the velocity of circulation of money that can be different for cash deposits held in the banking system and for coins and notes in circulation (base money created by the central bank).

The Dynamics of Changes in the Value of Money

Understanding the causes of fluctuations in the value of money was a main theme in Fisher, Wicksell, Pigou and, of course, Keynes. Book IV (Volume I) of the TM explores "The Dynamics of the Price Level". Adding to the classification of bank deposits made in Chapter 3 (income deposits, business deposits, savings deposits), JMK provides in Volume II a new classification of the total quantity of money distinguishing between deposits oriented to *Industry,* say activities of production, distribution and exchange and the payments of the factors of production and deposits that are channelled to *Finance* related to the holding and exchange of existing titles of wealth traded in the stock exchange and money market, speculation and the transfer of savings and profits into the hands of entrepreneurs.

In general, "money devoted to industry" (the real sector of the economy) corresponds to income deposits and part of business deposits in checking accounts; in turn, "money devoted to finance" corresponds, mainly, to savings deposits (terminology used in the UK) or time deposits (terminology in the USA). Both circuits compete in attracting money in circulation. Speculative operations (acquisition of securities) can displace money going to capital formation or be used for working capital and inventories in the production side of the economy. The old distinction between economic resources that go to the financial sphere versus resources devoted to actual production is also present in the *Treatise*. Here we can see a sort of correspondence between money held for the *finance motive* – "the bearish versus the bullish" of the *Treatise* – and the *speculative motive* for holding money (one of the three motives of the demand for money) formulated in the *General Theory*.[7]

The stability of the ratios of savings deposits and cash deposits to total deposits is related to the degree of optimism (or pessimism) reigning in financial markets. Confidence level or "*opinion*", regarding the overall economy and reflected in the price of securities, is a key ingredient of the "credit cycle". A "bear market" is characterised by the selling of securities short and a preference for holding cash. In contrast, in a "bullish market", people prefer to hold securities and borrow cash. In the markets of the real world, it may coexist with both a group of people with a bull outlook and another group adopting bear positions. Expectations can be heterogeneous across individuals with different consequences for the holdings of money in terms of cash deposits and savings deposits.

Dominant "bear" positions or, alternatively, "bullish" market positions may lead to declines or increases in the supply of money available to industry (the enterprise sector in charge of production and employment creation) producing ups and downs in the price level, leading to oscillations in the value of money. The state of financial expectations affects the price level through this monetary/financial mechanism and through the attractiveness of investment.

The central bank, *operating indirectly* through the bank rate, can regulate the supply of money and the availability of credit to industry and finance to avoid wild fluctuations in the price level and output. However, this management of liquidity by monetary authorities can be complicated by the degree of bullish and bear sentiments in financial markets. Ideally, JMK advocates that the monetary authorities must induce an adjustment in the market interest rate to make investment equal to savings and avoid a disequilibrium that pressures prices upwards or downwards (essentially a Wicksellian criteria). This may not be easy to accomplish as monetary authorities act through *indirect instruments* that affect the stock of money, and at the same time, the demand for money fluctuates according to the complex laws of the formation of expectations. The demand for money may fall if people shift to interest-bearing financial assets following bullish positions in which the appetite for risk taking is higher. Conversely, people may seek refuge in money when they are in a bearish position with less appetite for risk. As in the *Tract on Monetary Reform*, Keynes' preference in the TM is for an accommodative monetary policy in which the supply of money adjusts to shifts in the demand for money.

Causes of a Disequilibrium of Purchasing Power: Monetary Factors and Investment

Chapter 16, using the framework of the fundamental equations, concentrates on two types of disturbances affecting the price level:

1 Changes due to monetary factors
2 Changes due to investment factors

The *monetary factors* affect the price level through two channels: the I-S/O term – demand push effects – and, indirectly, through the E/O (costs of production) term – cost-push effects – in the price level equation. JMK warned that monetary policy is a particularly *ill-suited mechanism* to combat inflation whose origin is cost pressures, say "income inflation", since to reduce wages an increase in the interest rate must depress investment and create a recession causing unemployment that is socially and humanely costly. He was critical of what, nowadays, we call "austerity policies" or "shock treatment" that seek to *increase unemployment* to push down wages and prices to boost competitiveness. Unsurprisingly, the main representatives of the pro-austerity stance in Britain were the Treasury (Ministry of Finance) and the Bank of England, two powerful economic institutions, with which JMK held constant polemics.

Relying on austerity is a consequence that in a market economy, the state cannot decree a reduction in monetary wages paid in the private sector – and it is politically difficult to do it also with employees of the public sector – so it is left to the monetary policy acting in an *indirect* way to push nominal wages down through an increase in unemployment that reduces the bargaining power of labour and pressures wages down. The problem of the 1920s was that the downward wage flexibility that may have operated in the 19th century was largely inoperative due to the strengthening of labour unions and the capacity of wage resistance by workers who refused to accept cuts in their nominal wages.

Conversely, interest rates tend to work better, argued JMK, to combat "profit inflation" originated in an imbalance between I and S (disequilibrium in the commodities market) as higher interest rates will certainly discourage investment and promote, somewhat, savings.

As mentioned before, the *investment channel* was very important to Keynes to create wealth and prosperity:

> If enterprise is afoot, wealth accumulates whatever may be happening to thrift [savings]; and if enterprise is asleep, wealth decays whatever thrift may be doing.
>
> (Book VI, p. 132)

The accomplishments of modern civilisation such as large cities, technical innovations and discoveries, the railways system and the shipping industry that connects the world are often the result of actions by adventurous, enterprising people – the entrepreneur – rather than by passive savers, like to stress JMK in his various writings and, of course, in the *Treatise*.

Another main message is of a psychological type: investment is more driven by "animal spirits" (an urge to act) rather than by cold calculations of costs and benefits under conditions of certainty and full knowledge of the future. Although thrift and frugality were exalted by different writers in the 19th century as key virtues of capitalism, they do not play an *active* role in *igniting* progress and prosperity. Capital accumulation and innovation are the driving force to stimulate economic growth and prosperity.

Another related theme is the *coordination problem* present in a multi-agent, complex capitalist economy among those who make capital investments and those who provide the savings. The difficulties bringing in line those two different sets of decisions lie at the heart of fluctuations and crises in the economy.[8]

The *Treatise* looks at investment factors that drive a business cycle and the process of price dynamics. To avoid confusing an *autonomous* change in investment with an *induced* change – originated in monetary factors and interest rates changes – Keynes offers a list of factors that stimulate investment *independent* from a change in the interest rate related to monetary policy:

- Technical innovations (e.g., the discovery of electricity and internal-combustion engine),
- Needs of capital because of demographic trends (e.g., a shortage of houses and roads that need to be built) or the discovery of new valuable minerals (e.g., gold and diamonds). The role of technical innovations in spurring investment was stressed, particularly, by Joseph Schumpeter.
- Changes in confidence, sentiment or opinion in the investment community can also lead to an increase (or fall) in investment; these changes are related to psychological factors.

The *Treatise* estimates that about three-quarters of total investment is in fixed capital, say long-lived assets such as buildings, railways and other infrastructure. Therefore, the *long-run interest rate* is the relevant variable for this component of fixed capital formation. In turn, short-term interest rates could be more relevant for affecting working capital and stocks of goods investments.

In the *Treatise*, JMK relies strongly on the concept of *credit cycles* to understand imbalances between investment and savings emphasising the role of the banking system in attempting to make compatible the savings and investment decisions made by different sets of individuals, a task that is not guaranteed by changes in the interest rate. In contrast with his fellows' economists, JMK always emphasised that the "savings function" and the "investment function" have different determinants in a capitalist economy.

The first phase of the credit cycle can lead to an accommodation of an increase in investment demand (changes in savings are assumed to be less frequent) by an increase in credit, conducive to "commodity/profit inflation" and a windfall of profits. The second phase may involve a period of "income inflation" related to increases in wages and other costs of production. Prices will rise following the increase in the costs of production. A third and collapsing phase in the credit cycle will entail a closing of the excess of investment over savings and, consequently, to windfall losses. In these phases, prices fall and possibly production wiping out windfall profits generated in the previous phases of the cycle. These changes induce a shift in financial sentiment – or opinion and confidence – in the direction of a "bear market" that will show up in an increase in the demand for money. The initial stimulus to investment disappears and the economy transits from boom to recession.

In the GT, a fall in investment leads to a slump (fall of output and employment) but in the *Treatise* the end of the credit cycle leads to price deflation (with some adjustment also taking place in output). Regarding monetary factors underlying the credit cycle, there is a discrepancy between the market interest rate and the natural interest rate. If both rates were equal, there would be no credit cycle at all as investment and savings would be equal. Chapters 19 and 20 elaborate further on the credit cycle with some algebraic formalisations along the way. It is interesting to note that, implicitly, credit is an *endogenous* variable following the mismatches between investment and savings. An exogenous credit boom is not in the spirit of the *Treatise*.

Chapter 21 is the last of Volume I (on the theory of money) and focuses on the issue of international disequilibrium in an economy integrated into the rest of the world by trade in goods and services and movements of capital among nations. Analytically, the international economy affects the domestic economy through two main channels: relative price levels that affect the foreign (trade) balance and relative interest rates that govern foreign lending. The interaction of both determines the balance of payments settled by variations in the stock of gold. Keynes worked out various themes involving adjustment in price levels among countries, adjustment in interest rates, the relative balances between savings and investment, application to the German transfer problem, polemics with Bertil Ohlin and amendments of equilibrium conditions for the equality in market interest rates across countries and equality in the natural interest rate.

Volume II. The Applied Theory of Money

Volume II of the Treaty is devoted to empirical and historical illustrations of the theories of Volume I and will not be analysed in detail here. It contains very insightful policy discussions reflecting the strong command that Keynes had on both monetary theories, the institutional framework of various countries and knowledge of history and actual policymaking.

Book I, Chapters 22–26, deals with "monetary factors and their fluctuations" covering proportions of savings deposits and cash deposits in the banking system, the velocity of circulation of bank money, ratios of bank money to reserve money and the activity of business. Book VI, chapters 27–30, focuses on the "fluctuations of investment" distinguishing the different behaviour of the various components of investment: fixed capital investment, working capital investment and liquid investment, all with historical illustrations of investment cycles of the Spanish Treasure, the depression of the 1890s, the 1914–1918 war boom and its aftermath, the experience of Great Britain's return to the gold standard, the United States in 1925–1930 and the "Gibson Paradox".

Textbox 4.1   The Gibson Paradox

The so-called Gibson paradox stated by Keynes in the *Treatise* refers to the empirical finding of a *positive* correlation between the yield of British Consols – a perpetual bond offered by the Bank of England – and the price level as measured by the Wholesale Price Index in a period of more than a century, dominated by the gold standard. The paradox was presented by the British economist Alfred Herbert Gibson in an article published in 1923. The "paradox" status of this finding stems from the fact that economists would expect a negative relation between prices and interest rates as tight money leads to high-interest rates reducing investment and effective demand in the economy leading to a downward effect on prices. Alternatively, a rise in interest rates can create an excess of savings over investment with deflationary effects on the price level.

Irving Fisher tried to resolve this dilemma by noting that nominal interest rates are equal to the real interest rate plus *expected inflation*, rather than the price level. An analysis of the Gibson paradox under the gold standard appears in Barsky and Summers (1988).

Book VII, Chapters 31–38, deals with "The Management of Money" at national and international levels comprising detailed and interesting chapters devoted to methods of regulating money creation by commercial banks, illustrated with actions of the Bank of England, The US Federal Reserve System and the Continental Europe banking system. The management and criteria of policies and reserves of the central bank, relations between central banks of different countries, the management of the gold standard as affecting central banks and member banks, how to maintain some degree of national autonomy in the conduct of monetary policy in the framework of the gold standard are all topics discussed with ample recourse to actual experiences and Keynes keen knowledge of monetary and banking matters. The volume closes with a discussion of the scope and limits of controlling investment and supra-national monetary management illustrated through the Bank of International Settlements in the first three decades of the 20th century.

Reactions and Comments to the *Treatise*

The publication of the *Treatise* in 1930 led to varied reactions by academic economists such as F. Hayek, D.H. Robertson and A. Hansen with replies by Maynard Keynes (he was rarely called by his first name).[9] These comments appeared mostly in leading economic journals in the United Kingdom. Hayek, for example, was critical of the definitions of savings, investment and profits used in the *Treatise*. In addition, he lamented that JMK did not use the rounda-bout production framework and the capital theory of Eugene Bohm-Bawerk, although JMK adopted in the *Treatise* the dual interest rate theory of Wicksell (a student of Bohm-Bawerk). Still, he refrained from identifying the natural interest rate with the marginal productivity of capital. The *Treatise* makes the demand for investment as a function of the interest rate and the effects of uncertainty. Further, his observations of the different types of investment and their determinants are quite insightful.

Alvin Hansen, later an active promoter of Keynes in America, pointed to shortcomings of the fundamental equations and pinpointed potential errors in results embedded in the TM.

Methodological Issues: Marshallian Equilibrium, Time and Adjustment Mechanisms

The adjustment to disequilibrium in the *Treatise of Money* is a *mixed story* of Alfred Marshall's (Keynes' professor) formulation of market adjustment and the market clearing process proposed by French economist Leon Walras. The Marshallian equilibrium was originally formulated for a single market or industry (see his *Principles of Economics*; Marshall, 1890 [1961]), but the analysis is extended by Keynes to the aggregate, macro level. In fact, in Marshall super-normal profits (difference between revenues and costs of production, the latter including a normal return to the entrepreneur) may ex-ist in the short-medium run in *industry*; however, these excess returns should eventually disappear when new producers enter the market, and the forces of competition and the new supply of output lead to lower prices, wiping out abnormal profits. Keynes extended the zero-profit condition of Marshall to the *macro equilibrium* when investment = savings.

At the same time, the fundamental price equations of the *Treatise* choose the price level as the adjustment variable to correct the imbalances between savings and investment (or excess demand/supply in the goods market). In that sense, it resembles the Walras formulation in which excess demand func-tions (demand minus supply at a given price) are corrected through upward and downward adjustments in *prices*. In general equilibrium, a vector of equi-librium relative prices clear, simultaneously, the different markets that com-pose an economy. Summing up, Keynes in the *Treatise* provides a *hybrid story* of Marshallian zero-profit equilibrium combined with a price-based Walrasian market clearing mechanism.

The issue of the *time dimension* of the analysis is studied in Amadeo's (1989) analysis of the *Treatise of Money*. The author distinguishes between historical static (equilibrium positions) and historical dynamic (transitions between equilibrium positions) and argues that the *Treatise* admits both possibilities.

This is not the only possible formulation of time in economics. Joan Robinson, once, made the distinction between *historical time* and *logical time* and warned that once an economy is out of equilibrium, there is no guarantee that it will reach a new equilibrium as expectations may be falsified during the dynamic process and history rules. The Treatise adopts "the production period analysis", which is the time that elapses between the levels of output and employment decided by the firm, and the goods are produced and taken to the market and sold at a given price (or remain unsold and accumulate as inventories or *liquid capital* in the terminology of the *Treatise*). In the production period, output and employment are given but this does not necessarily mean that output is fixed at full employment. The TM also works with a *sequence of production periods* in which changes in prices, output, employment, investment and savings take place.

The *Treatise* adopts, implicitly, the position that equilibrium tends to be stable around a trajectory of full utilisation of labour and capital although admitting oscillations and disequilibrium positions. This is the main point of the "fundamental equations" with imbalances between investment and savings. But, the zero-profit equilibrium is stable. Credit cycles can occur but, eventually, they will be phased away in equilibrium.

The adjustment mechanism – which variable solves a saving-investment imbalance – is also a complex issue in which the interpretations of Keynes tend *not* to coincide, strictly, with what JMK *wrote* in the *Treatise* and the *General Theory*. The conventional story of Hicks, Patinkin and Leijonhufvud is that while the *Treatise* is a book focused on price adjustment, the *General Theory* is a quantity (income, employment)-adjustment book in which two different variables – prices or quantities – vary in reaction to imbalances between investment and savings.

However, the reader of *Treatise* and *The General Theory* will find Keynes' descriptions are in terms of *both* output and employment *and* the price level. For example, Keynes in the GT mentions in Chapter 19 and other places that price and income *both* adjust to a change in effective demand and that the assumption of a horizontal aggregate supply curve is not realistic. The fixed price interpretation can be a useful analytical approximation for understanding and the teaching of Keynesian economics but is not exactly what Keynes said in the *General Theory*.

The mechanism of *forced savings* is also present in the *Treatise*. It operates in the following way: when investment exceeds savings, prices rise, reducing the purchasing power of those earning a fixed nominal income (in the relevant production period). The result is a reduction in consumption or, its counterpart, an increase in savings for a given level of output. The savings increase is "forced" by the adjustment in the price level and serves the purpose of aligning savings with investment to restore macroeconomic equilibrium. In this context, actual savings is the sum of desired savings and forced savings.[10] The extent of the forced savings will depend on the size of the imbalance between planned investment and desired savings, the response of the price level and the degree of "wage rigidity". Later, Nicholas Kaldor rescued the notion of David Ricardo that the average propensity to save out of capital incomes is greater than the average propensity to save of wage incomes to show that a price-driven redistribution from wage-earners to profit earners will drive up overall (private) savings in line with the forced savings mechanism just described. Here we add a change in functional income distribution to the adjustment variables of prices and quantities.

Economic Policy Objectives

The *Treatise* implicit policy view was that by ensuring price stability, automatically, there will be a tendency for economic fluctuations to dampen, and the economy will approach full employment of labour and capital. A similar view is adopted, broadly, in the *Tract*. In this approach, there are no apparent trade-offs between price stability and full employment, the trademark of the original Phillips curve. Later, with the Friedman and Phelps vertical Phillips curve formulation, the trade-off vanishes, and money is neutral in line with quantity theory predictions. In these conditions, the trade-off between price stability and unemployment simply disappears.

Treatise's Book III and Book IV try to disengage themselves from the quantity of money approach and elaborate a theory of disequilibrium in prices. Nevertheless, no apparent trade-off explicitly emerges between price stability and full employment. Both objectives become, apparently, complementary with no policy dilemmas and *no trade-offs* between price stability and full employment.

Other policy trade-offs and dilemmas, however, emerge in the *Treatise*. Chief among them is the recognition that under the gold standard and free capital mobility among nations the degree of national autonomy to carry monetary policy for an individual country can be severely impaired, particularly in small economies. Also, domestic inflation cannot diverge for long from international inflation in a world of fixed exchange rates (gold standard system); otherwise, exports will diminish, and imports will increase creating a trade deficit in the balance of payments due to a loss in external competitiveness. Likewise, domestic interest rates (adjusted by expected currency depreciation) and international interest rates must converge; otherwise, capital inflows will go to the high-interest rate country, increasing the gold supply in the recipient country and diminishing it in the origin country. The conclusion is clear: an economy that is integrated internationally in both the goods market and the capital market may face conflicts between the attainment of internal balance and external balance. External openness not only brings economic benefits to the trading economies but also imposes macroeconomic restrictions.

The Monetary-Financial Mechanism of the *Treatise*

The monetary theory of the *Treatise* is one in which the banking system plays a fundamental dual role in both the provision of liquidity to the economy and the support – through credit – of industry (production) and finance (acquisition of securities such as stocks and bonds). The banks, on the one hand, provide liquidity through the creation of bank money (checking accounts). Banks also act as clearinghouses transferring liquidity between individuals, firms and other banks. This process of liquidity provision is like the *lifeblood* of the economic system; the circulation of money must proceed as smoothly as possible to avoid blockades and interruptions in normal economic life. On the other hand, banks provide credit to finance fixed investment (long-term loans), working capital investment and liquid investment (short- and medium-term loans). The different types of loans carry different interest rates forming an array of interest rates with a different term structure.

The central bank, in turn, regulates the amount of bank money that commercial banks can create and the liquidity of the economy through four channels: (i) the value of the bank rate that prices the cost of discount operations, (ii) through open market operations, (iii) regulation of reserve ratios and (iv) the general purchase of assets including gold.

The TM establishes a distinction between "financial circulation" (money channelled to finance the acquisition of securities) and "industry circulation" (money channelled to finance production and distribution). Both compete for a given level of deposits in the banking system. Special attention is given to the proportion of deposits held as cash deposits or maintained as savings deposits. The latter is closer to financial circulation and the former is closer to industry circulation. In turn, bank money has a different velocity of circulation than the velocity of circulation of high-power money: coins and banknotes. The *Treatise* taxonomy of income deposits (held by households) and business deposits (held by productive units) that hold cash deposits underscore different velocities of circulation. The concept of velocity, so central to the quantity theory, is more relevant to the concept of cash deposits in the banking system, argues Keynes. Originally, the concept of velocity referred more to the speed of circulation of coins and notes but in more recent times must be adjusted to fit the circulation of cash deposits in the banks.

In a predominantly banking economy with a large proportion of the total money held in bank cash deposits, Keynes develops a formula for the turnover of the cash deposits (velocity of circulation), tied to the "efficiency" of the total deposits defined as the ratio of bank clearings to total deposits. A further separation is between "the velocity of income deposits" and "the velocity of business deposits" (see Vol. II, Chapter 24, pp. 22–23). This institutional detail was largely abandoned, later, in the *General Theory*.

Credit/business cycles are related to changing proportions of credit going to finance the production of consumer goods and the production of investment goods in line with the imbalance between savings and investment.

Shifts between "bear" and "bullish" attitudes by investors affect the price of securities (falling for bears and rising for bulls) in the phases of the trade cycle. The final phase of a collapse occurs when investment sharply declines, and a bear market sets in. It is apparent that the credit cycle is *not* a theory in which *autonomous or exogenous* change in the stock of credit provided by the banking system is what creates a business cycle. In line with Wicksell, credit varies *endogenously* in response to the excess of investment to savings (of either sign).

The role of the banking system, influenced by the central bank or monetary authority, is to help to restore an equilibrium between flows of savings and investment with investment bearing most of the adjustment.

The transmission vehicle between the stock of money – dominated by bank money (demand deposits and checking accounts) rather than coins and banknotes – is the market interest determined in the loan market. Inspired by the Wicksell story of the loanable investment market for JMK, the disequilibrium between investment and savings will vanish only when the market interest rate equals the natural interest rate.

For Wicksell, the natural rate is equal to the marginal productivity of capital (MPK). If the market rate is below the MPK, the cost of borrowing will be lower than the return on borrowed funds so the demand for loans will be greater than the supply of loans. Conversely, if MPK is below the interest rate, the profitability of capital is lower than the cost of funds, and the demand for funds will shrink compared with the supply of loans. In Wicksell, the price level moves upward and downward according to the sign of the imbalance in the loanable funds market.

The MPK concept is not used in the *Treatise* as just mentioned. The analysis is conducted more in terms of differences between the expected return of investment and the interest rate; the issue is developed more fully in the *General Theory* under the name of "marginal efficiency of investment". Importantly, the marginal efficiency of capital (the expected present discounted value of future profits) is not the same thing as the marginal productivity of capital.

JMK assumed that interest rates affect the demand for investment more than the supply of savings. Accordingly, Volume I (theory/qualitative) and

Volume II (application/quantitative, empirical and historical) are devoted to study the fluctuations in investment. In contrast, virtually no chapter of the *Treatise* is devoted to the study of the fluctuations of savings.

Notes

1 See Kahn (1984).
2 The dual price level structure stressed in Minsky (1975 [2008]).
3 With M = stock of money, V = velocity of circulation, P = price level, O = output following the *Treatise* notation of the variables.
4 See p. 136. The wages rate as the first argument assumes, for simplicity, labour is the only factor of production. Therefore, factor earnings correspond to labour earnings (= the wage rate, at efficiency).
5 A second-round effect follows that the cut in prices reduces entrepreneurial remuneration and employment exerting a downward pressure on wages and the cost of production (the "earnings of the factors of production" in TM terminology) until a new equilibrium is achieved (with wages and prices falling in the same proportion in line with neutrality of nominal variables).
6 JMK makes a qualification on the definition of the bank rate in the Section "The General Theory of the Bank Rate" (p. 200). Here the bank rate is defined as the effective (actual) market interest rate for lending and borrowing that prevails in the market and not necessarily the official central bank rate to discount paper. It is an array of interest rates effective in the market at any time for the borrowing and lending of money for short periods.
7 For this interpretation, see Kahn (1984), Fifth Lecture, Section "Liquidity Preference", p. 141.
8 The Swedish economist Axel Leijonhufvud (Leijonhufvud, 1968) stressed the role of *coordination failures* in macroeconomic analysis.
9 Hayek (1931, 1932), Keynes (1931) and Hansen (1932).
10 See Amadeo (1989, ch.3, pp. 43–44).

5 The General Theory of Employment, Interest and Money

A New Macroeconomics of Depression

Practical men, who believe they to be quite exempt from any intellectual influences, are usually the slaves of some defunct economist. Madmen in authority, who hear voices in the air, are distilling their frenzy from some academic scribbler of a few years back.

(Keynes, 1964 [1936], p. 12)

Keynes' most famous book, *The General Theory of Interest, Income and Employment* (GT), started to be written in 1931, shortly after finishing the *Treatise,* and it was published in 1936. It is said Keynes was not entirely pleased with the *Treatise*. Moreover, there was an urgent need to have a theory consistent with an economy stuck in a prolonged slump featuring high unemployment and unused capital. The TM was a book more preoccupied with the price level.

Indeed, JMK incorporated some of his new ideas articulated in the TM into the GT; others, he radically modified. While the GT does discuss critical issues affecting public policy – from macroeconomic theory to the nature of human psychology and decisions under intractable uncertainty – JMK wrote the GT in his heart for "my fellow economists."

The genesis of this important book comprised several pieces of work that involved Keynes, his students and some colleagues.

In an article written in 1929 by J.M. Keynes and D. Henderson entitled *Can Lloyd George Do It?*, the authors examine the liberal party manifesto of 1929, *We Can Conquer Unemployment,* prepared for the general elections of that year in Britain. Keynes and Henderson endorsed the proposed programme of public works of the liberal party oriented to reduce unemployment in Britain that reached 1.14 million people in April of 1929 and that had remained around 10 percent of the labor force for several years.

They argue that this programme would create additional purchasing power *above* the value of the programme as employment creation would pay wages to workers that would be used in consumption, stimulating the production of the consumer goods industry and other related industries, creating new incomes

DOI: 10.4324/9781003480785-5

throughout the economy. An additional bonus of this virtuous cycle is the extra revenues to the Treasury and the savings in benefits payments to the unemployed who were financed out of a government-sponsored "Unemployment Fund"'. To work out in rigorous mathematical terms the total *direct* and *indirect* employment and income effects from an expansion in public investment, Keynes asked his former student and now young colleague, Richard Kahn, to develop a more thorough calculation. The result was an article entitled "The Relation of Home Investment to Unemployment" published in *The Economic Journal* in June 1931. Thus, the real father of the "multiplier" was Richard Kahn. Keynes would use it, recognising the authorship of Khan, and the concept and formula became important pieces of the *General Theory*'s analytical apparatus. Kahn's own description on the development of the multiplier (Kahn, 1984, Fourth Lecture, From the "multiplier" to the General Theory) shows how it was related to Keynes' and Henderson's article including the need to clarify direct and indirect employment effects with the second associated with the propensity of consume. In addition, Kahn's description includes the role of the Cambridge "Circus", say a group of then-younger Cambridge economists who were colleagues of Keynes comprising James Meade, Joan and Austin Robinson, Piero Sraffa and Richard Kahn in clarifying implications from the multiplier analysis for output determination and the role of investment.

In a nutshell, the multiplier shows that an exogenous increase in public spending had first, second and near-infinite round effects on employment and income. However, these effects *decreased* over time, eventually turning very small; in mathematical terms, the progression was a *converging* geometric series. Kahn showed that the total effect of a fiscal expansion was the size of the increase in public investment times 1/1-MPC (the multiplier) in which MPC is the marginal propensity to consume, dC/dY. For the stability condition of the geometric series, the marginal propensity to consume lies in the interval between 0 and 1.

Another motivation for the *General Theory* was to further develop the theory of money. It is said that the GT was, originally, to be entitled "A Monetary Theory of Production". In fact, this is the name of Keynes' article published in 1933 which laid the basis for a monetary analysis going beyond the *neutrality of money*. Eventually, the GT created a role for money and specified the mechanisms through which the supply of money affects the volume of output and employment in an economy that is different from a "real-exchange economy" in which money is only a device to economise transaction costs of a barter economy that need for double coincidence of goods to materialise transactions. In an economy in which money is non-neutral, it can affect the real side of the economy (production and employment).

In his words:

Now, the conditions required for the "neutrality" of money, in the sense which this is assumed ...are, I suspect, precisely the same as those which will ensure that crises *do not occur*. If this is true, the real-exchange economics, on which most of us have been brought up ...is a singularly blunt weapon for dealing with the problem of booms and depressions. For it has assumed away the very matter under investigation... Accordingly, I believe that the next task is to work out in some detail a monetary theory of production, to supplement the real-exchange theories which we already possess. At any rate this is the task on which I am now occupying myself, in some confidence that I am not wasting my time.

(The Essential Keynes, EK, p. 176)

In the Preface to the *General Theory*, JMK describes the process more explicitly:

When I began to write my *Treatise on Money* I was still moving along the traditional lines regarding the influence of money as something so to speak separate from the general theory of supply and demand. When I finished it, I had made some progress towards pushing monetary theory back to becoming a theory of output as a whole.

(The Essential Keynes, p. 177)

In a letter to Roy Harrod on 30 August 1936, JMK stated that:

To me the most extraordinary thing regarded historically is the complete disappearance of the theory of demand and supply for output as a whole, i.e. the theory of employment, after it had been for a quarter of century the most discussed thing in economics. One of the most important transitions for me, after my *Treatise on Money* had been published, was suddenly realising this.

(EK, p. 177)

These paragraphs suggest at least three important issues:

i   The quantity theory and the real-exchange economy approach leave virtually no room for money to affect real economic activity.
ii The demand and supply framework so central in "the theory of value" used in microeconomic analysis (prevailing at the time the GT was published) was not applied to macroeconomic analysis, say the analysis of a whole economy rather than a particular industry.
iii Money affects prices and quantities through interest rates and aggregate demand.

A key innovation of the *General Theory* was the *principle of effective demand*, viewed as the main determinant of the level of aggregate economic activity acting through several steps that we shall identify in this chapter.

Textbox 5.1   The Walras Law and the Say's Law

The Walras law states that the sum of the excess demand of individual markets in the economy must be zero (independent of the prices, of equilibrium or disequilibrium, in each market). This implies that if some markets are in excess supply, other markets will be in excess demand. This property follows from the aggregation of the budget constraints of the different agents of the economy. Walras law states that if there are n markets in the economy, then only $n-1$ markets are *independent equations* to determine equilibrium money prices. Then, if we have $n-1$ commodities that are in equilibrium (the excess demand functions are zero at a given price vector), then the money market, the nth market, will also be in equilibrium. Other combinations of markets are possible: for example, the labour market, the commodity market (as an aggregate) and the bond market. The Walras law was developed by the French economist Leon Walras in his book *Elements of Pure Economics* of 1874. The set of equilibrium prices in Walras formulation is solved by a method of successive approximations – the *tatonnement* – that iterate until all markets are cleared (net excess demand functions are zero in general equilibrium). The term "Walras law" was coined by the Polish economist Oskar Lange to distinguish it from Say's law.[1] For Lange, both laws will coincide only in an economy without money and in full general equilibrium.

Say's law was formulated by the economist Jean Baptiste Say in *A Treatise on Political Economy*, 1834 (the original in French was published in 1803). It states that there cannot be an excess supply in the economy as trade is a reciprocal exchange in which all goods produced are ultimately consumed. The Say law, that Keynes, Marx and others criticised, is challenged in a monetary economy in which people are paid in monetary wages and not in goods as would be the case in a barter economy. Therefore, individuals after receiving their money income as payment for their work may decide to *spend less* than what they earn by hoarding (saving) money. This breaks the equivalence between production and spending (Say's law) and can be a cause of deficiency of effective demand in the economy. Sometimes, there is a mention of the "Keynes law" in which aggregate demand determines output, reversing Say's law in which supply creates its own demand.

A curious omission of the *General Theory*, in sharp contrast with the *Tract* and the *Treatise,* is the absence in the analysis of the banking system and its integration into the loan market, and the investment and savings process. This should not be interpreted, however, as meaning that Keynes was not aware of the importance of banking in the period preceding the publication of the GT. In fact, in 1932, he wrote an article "The Consequences to the Banks of the Collapse of Money Values" motivated by the collapse of (large) banks that took place in Austria (Credit Anstalt), Germany (Darmstadter) and the crises of many local and regional banks that had lent heavily to farmers in the United States between 1929 and 1933 (see Chapter 2 of this book).

In the 1932 article, JMK analysed the effects of the decline in the price of bonds, property, land, stocks on the net worth of banks and their willingness to keep providing credits. In addition, the impact of an adverse "wealth effect" associated with declining asset prices impairs the capacity of borrowers to serve their outstanding debts. Perhaps a reason why Keynes did not incorporate the banking system (and central banks) in the *General Theory* was to avoid diverting readers' attention from the variables that formed the central elements of the new book: the principle of effective demand, the propensity to consume, the investment function, the theory of preference for liquidity and the role of uncertainty.

The behaviour of investment, like in the *Treatise,* is a central theme in the *General Theory*. This includes the intrinsic difficulties in anticipating future yields due to the existence of inescapable uncertainty and the changes in the marginal efficiency of capital due to the effects of the interest rate on capital formation.

GT's writing style combines Keynes's gifts for vivid literary exposition with only a moderate use (by today's standards) of equations, calculus and algebra. Still, the GT does not always render for absolute clarity and some chapters can be obtrusive and demanding. Subsequent clarifications and mathematical formalisations by John Hicks, Franco Modigliani, Paul Samuelson, Don Patinkin, Axel Leijonhufvud and others – generally casting JMK in equilibrium analysis – have made the GT more comprehensible for students of economics trained in formal analysis. However, formalisations and simplifications have the cost of not necessarily reflecting all the richness and complexity of the original text.

As documented, Keynes was not an Ivory Tower academic but someone aware of the turns, tricks and ways of the real world. He entertained the notion of the social responsibility of the economist in making the world a better place to live and to help avoid crises and human suffering. An ethical concern on informing better policies that can improve the living material conditions of the common citizen permeates the book. It is a polemical book at times, and mostly lively, insightful and penetrating.

The main themes and results of the GT can be advanced as follows:

i   The "normal state" of a capitalist economy is one in which labour is un-
    deremployed (there is persistent unemployment) and capital is underuti-
    lised (excess capacity of machinery, equipment and structures) rather than
    one in which resources are being fully employed.

ii Effective demand defined as the sum of aggregate consumption and in-
    vestment (closed economy) determines output, real incomes and employ-
    ment in the aggregate (in the whole economy). Say's law in which supply
    creates its own demand is dispensed with.

iii The propensity to consume, the preference for liquidity, the inducement to
    investment and the multiplier are the key variables in driving macroeco-
    nomic equilibrium.

iv An under-employment equilibrium can be particularly stable. It is un-
    likely that it will be automatically corrected by adjustment in the interest
    rate, wages and prices as stated in the classic tradition.

v   Investors, entrepreneurs, consumers and asset holders face fundamental
    or irreducible uncertainty. Their economic decisions are often made under
    conditions of flimsy, fragmentary and limited information. Mass psychol-
    ogy, driven at least in part by "ignorance and the dark forces of time",
    plays a significant role in forming expectations on which investment and
    financial decisions are made. In uncertain contexts, economic agents al-
    locate time and resources to anticipate average opinions of fellow par-
    ticipants in the market for equities and other securities rather than devote
    their energies to anticipate the long-run yields of physical investment.

As Keynes himself posits in the first page of the *General Theory*, the
prefix "General" in the title of the book was precisely aimed to show that
the *most observed* situation of a capitalist economy is of *underemployment*
of labour and under-utilisation of capital. In adherence with the principle
of effective demand, the main notion is that the level of economic activity
is driven by consumption and investment.

Fiscal and monetary intervention by the government will be necessary
to mitigate the adverse effects of slumps and stagnation traps and help to
restore full employment. JMK was sceptical that private markets and individual investors, alone, would be able to pull an economy from a depressive equilibrium of the magnitude that took place around the world
between 1929 and 1933. Weak tendencies for automatic adjustment and
self-correction of large-scale disequilibria – a market failure – must be
counteracted by sensible and resolute government action. That was the
main message of the *General Theory*.

JMK was sceptical also that monetary policy would be an effective
weapon to combat a slump in the context of low-interest rates as was the
case in the 1930s. More effective could be direct injections of purchasing

power to the circular flow through investment in public works funded by the Treasury. Money acts *indirectly* on effective demand through interest rates and the marginal efficiency of capital, MEC, postulated JMK. A collapse in the MEC – triggered by obscure causes linked to the pretence of conventional knowledge in conditions of fundamental uncertainty – can take time to be reversed, particularly during a severe slump. Further, the remedy of lower interest rates may be too weak a medicine for a phenomenon hard to understand in its origin.

A main source of macroeconomic fluctuations is private investment whose behaviour is linked to the *unknown future* through anticipations of future yields, a theme developed in JMK's *Treatise of Probability*.

To make investment decisions under uncertainty requires, simply, acting based on the best information available. As said the "animal spirits" to some extent replace an almost impossible monetary calculation of costs and benefits of a stream of expenses and revenues of an enterprise (endowed with durable capital goods) several years ahead of time.

A Tour through the Book

The GT is organised around six "books": Book I (Introduction), Book II (Definition and Ideas), Book III (The Propensity to Consume), Book IV (The Inducement to Invest), Book V (Money – Wages and Prices) and Book VI (Short Notes Suggested by the General Theory).

Keynes presented a new theory that departs from the macroeconomics of the "classics" who were identified as "post-Ricardian" economists such as Edgeworth, Mill, Marshall and Professor Pigou. This is not the only definition of the classics. For Marx "classical political economy" referred to David Ricardo, John Stuart Mill and predecessors (see GT, footnote 1, p. 3).

In Book I, it is explained that the focus of the *General Theory* is on explaining the *scale and variation in (aggregate) income and employment*. In contrast, in the *Tract* and the *Treatise,* the focus was the price level (or the value of money).

In Book I, JMK abandons Say's law and the classic's treatment of the labour market as a market not very different from the market of apples and oranges governed by the forces of demand and supply. For the "classics", the competition among workers to get available jobs would induce them to accept lower wages offered by firms in a situation of unemployment. The forces of competition in the labour market would not be different from the forces of competition in markets for goods. Wage resistance, class solidarity and the reluctance to accept wage cuts by workers were issues largely neglected by the "classics". In this context, there can be only "frictional" or "voluntary unemployment" (see Chapter 2 of the GT). In the competitive labour market equilibrium, the real wage is equal *both* to the marginal productivity of labour (demand for labour) and the marginal disutility of work (supply of labour).

Keynes introduced the concept of *involuntary unemployment*. This notion was completely absent in Pigou's book *The Theory of Unemployment,* popular at that time. When there is involuntary unemployment, the real wage is *higher* than the marginal disutility of work: workers would be willing to work more at the prevailing real wage, but they just cannot find jobs.

In the frame of the *General Theory*, effective demand becomes the main determinant of aggregate employment (not the marginal conditions of the classic labour market theory). The aggregate supply function is solved for the level of employment. The equality between real wages, marginal productivity of labour and the marginal disutility of work is abandoned as an equilibrium condition. Output and employment are *not* determined by the supply side. Say's law goes out and is replaced by the principle of effective demand.

Box 5.2   Origins of the Concept of Effective Demand and Under-consumption: De Sismondi, Marx, Hobson, Luxembourg

Keynes did not really invent the macro concept of lack of consumer purchasing power or "deficit of effective demand". Theories of under-consumption, related to a lack of effective demand, come from the Swiss writer, economist and historian Sismondi de Sismondi (1773–1842) who was one of the first to coin the terms overproduction, capital accumulation and minimum/low wages used after in economics. Karl Marx rejected Say's law leading to a focus on effective demand and partially adopted the ideas of under-consumption/over-production associated with Sismondi as one cause of slumps in a capitalist economy (Marx, Engels and Lenin considered Sismondi a "romantic socialist"). Under-consumption was only one cause of a recessive cycle for Marx, and the others were the falling rate of profits and disproportionalities between the sectors producing consumption goods and capital goods.

Early in the 20th century, the Russian economist Tugan-Baranovsky and the Polish Rosa Luxemburg also elaborated further on the role of effective demand in capitalism's tendencies to experience recessions and booms. Independently, the Polish economist Michal Kalecki in the 1930s also developed a theory of economic cycles focused on effective demand composed by consumption of workers and investment of the capitalists. Kalecki, in turn, criticised aspects of the theories of effective demand of Tugan-Baranovsky and Rosa Luxembourg.[2] At the turn of the 20th century, also, the British liberal analyst John Hobson constructed a theory of imperialism based on the export of capital because of a limited local consumer market based on under-consumption. The notion of imperialism, the export of capital, economic cartels and inter country rivalries was explored further by Vladimir Lenin.[3]

Book II addresses the choice of units of the analysis (Chapter 4), expectations and employment (Chapter 5), the definition of income, savings and investment (Chapter 6) and the meaning of savings and investment further considered (Chapter 7). The *choice of units* adopted in the GT is eclectic and varies across different variables. Monetary values are used for prices and (nominal) wages; the *wage units* say the number of hours worked in producing a certain quantity of goods is used for measuring output, consumption, investment and the demand for money (liquidity preference). The interest rate and the proportion of income consumed are pure numbers (or percentages). Apparently, Keynes avoided, in the *General Theory*, expressing all relevant variables in real terms due to prevailing criticism, at that time, to the use of index numbers, a point brought by Schumpeter (1954) *A History of Economic Analysis*, ch.8, 4(c).

The definition of Savings, S, is the difference between income, Y, and consumption, C.

Savings = Income – Consumption.

$S = Y - C$

In the standard textbook, the interpretation of the Keynesian system (*General Theory*) in which real income is demand-determined, savings, imports and taxes are "leakages" of purchasing power. They reduce the circular flow. On the other hand, investment (public and private), defined as an addition, in each time interval, to the capital stock and changes in inventories along with public consumption and exports are *injections* of purchasing power. They *expand* the circular flow. The identities of national accounts in a closed economy between income, Y, output, O, savings, and investment must be always equal ex-post. In contrast, *ex-ante* – say planned savings and desired investment can be different.

$Y = C + S,$
$O = C + I,$ therefore
$S = I$

Then if aggregate demand $AD = C + I + G$, the equilibrium level of income is given by $AD = Y = C + I + G$ (G = government expenditure). In graphic terms, this is shown in Figure 5.1 below as the "Keynesian cross":

As discussed in the Treatise, savings and investment are carried out by different agents with distinct motivations: savings by households (although there are also retained profits which amount to corporate savings) and investment by firms or corporations (and investment by households). A main issue in macroeconomics is how the plans of savers and investors are reconciled and made consistent among them. This is a coordination issue and controversies centre on what is the most relevant adjustment variable: prices, interest rates,

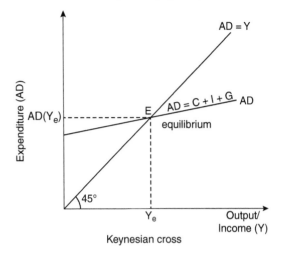

Figure 5.1 The Keynesian cross: output determination

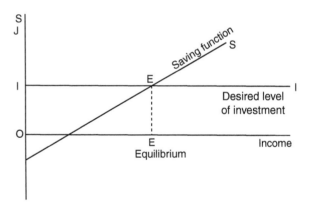

Figure 5.2 Saving investment equilibrium

output and employment to bring about the equality between planned investment and intended savings.

In the Keynes system of the General Theory, the income level is the one
that equilibrates savings with investment as depicted in Figure 5.2 in which
savings is a positive function of the level of income.[4]

Book III is devoted to the formulation of the "propensity to consume" that
depends on income – mediated by a marginal propensity to consume – related
to a set of "objective" factors (Chapter 8) such as income increases, windfall
gains, changes in time preference and a set of "subjective" factors (Chapter 9)

related to precaution, autonomy, enjoyment, liquidity, foresight and so on that are related to both consumption and savings motives. These definitions are more related to households, but Keynes also considered consumption and savings by enterprises and government.

Book IV is about the "inducement to invest". Keynes formulated the theory of investment around the concept of the *marginal efficiency of capital* (MEC) defined as the discount rate that equalises the present value of a stream of future profits – "annuities" in Keynes' terminology (see p. 135) – and the supply price of capital or replacement cost of investment. Keynes emphasised that expectations of future earnings "connect today and tomorrow" and that forming these expectations can be a tricky process due to uncertainty and the lack of knowledge of the future: the more distant is the future the more difficult it is to anticipate it.

The investment function can be written as:

$$I = f(r, MEC)$$

In which I = investment, r = the real interest rate, MEC = marginal efficiency of or present discounted value of future profits or annuities.

The GT alerts that undertaking a static, one period of analysis of current investment returns is unrealistic and of limited use. Uncertainty acts through the marginal efficiency of capital, understood also as the demand for investment (the supply of investment is given by the replacement cost schedule). The decision to invest will involve comparing the MEC with the *real interest rate*, which is defined as the nominal rate minus the "anticipated change in the value of money" in the terminology of Irving Fisher's *The Theory of Interest* (Fisher, 1930). The anticipated change in the value of money is, of course, the rate of *expected* inflation (reduction in the purchasing power of money) or deflation (increase in the real value of money).[5] The whole monetary analysis of the book is carried out in terms of market interest rates (no more market/ natural interest rate distinction).

Keynes prefers the term "real interest rate (nominal interest rate minus expected inflation)" rather than the terminology of "anticipations and interest" adopted by Fisher. An important point of the GT is that expectations of the future affect current equilibrium through two variables: the marginal efficiency of capital and expected real interest rates (and the comparison of the two).

Chapter 12 is devoted to explaining "Long-run Expectations" underscoring the complexities and ultimate futility of the belief that we can anticipate with certainty the future. The following paragraphs of the GT are very telling in that respect:

> The outstanding fact is the extreme precariousness of the basis of knowledge on which our expectations of yield. Our knowledge of the factors that govern the yield of an investment some years hence is usually very slight

and often negligible. If we speak frankly, we have to admit that our basis of knowledge for estimating the yield ten years hence of a railway, a copper mine, the goodwill of a patent medicine, an Atlantic liner, a building in the city of London amounts to little and sometimes nothing; or even five years hence.

...

In former times, when enterprises were owned by those who undertook them, or by their friends and associates, investment depended on a sufficient supply of individuals of sanguine temperament and constructive impulses who embarked on business as a way of life, not really relying on a precise calculation of prospective profits. The affair was partly a lottery though with the ultimate result largely governed by whether the abilities and character of the managers were above or below the average.

...

With the separation between owners and managers which prevails to-day and with the development of organised investment markets [the stock exchange market] a new factor of great importance has entered in, which sometimes facilitates investment but sometimes adds greatly to the instability of the system. In the absence of securities markets, there is no object in frequently attempting to revalue an investment to which we are committed. But the Stock Exchange revalues many investments every day... Thus, certain classes of investment are governed by the average expectation of those who deal on the stock exchange as revealed in the prices of shares rather than by the genuine expectation of the professional entrepreneur.

... "for most of these persons, are in fact largely concerned not with making superior long term forecasts of the probable yield of an investment over its whole life but with foreseen changes in the conventional basis of valuation a short time ahead of the general public. They are concerned not with what an investment is really worth to a man who buys it "for keeps" but with what the market will value it at, under the influence of mass psychology, three months from now or a year hence"... this is the inevitable result of organised investment markets organised with a view to so-called "liquidity". Of the maxims of orthodox finance, none, surely, is more anti-social than the fetish of liquidity, the doctrine that is a positive virtue on the part of investment institutions to concentrate their resources upon the holding of "liquid "securities. It suggests there is no such a thing as liquidity of investment for the community as a whole. The social object of skilled investors should be to defeat the dark forces of time and ignorance which envelope our future. The actual private object of the most skilled investment to-day is to "beat the gun "as Americans express it so well, to outwit the crowd, and to pass the bad, or depreciating, half-crown to the other fellow.

(GT, Book IV, pp. 149–152)

Several implications, some advanced before, can be derived from these quotations:

i   Investment is concerned with *future* earnings and future costs, but it is very difficult to have a *reliable estimate of future yields* of investment since knowledge of the future is, by definition, very limited.
ii Keynes although presented in the GT the relevant profitability equations to describe private "optimal" investment behaviour, he was, at the same time, aware of the limits of these calculations for actual investment behaviour in a world of uncertainty regarding the future and favoured "animal spirits" – rather than optimisation.
iii Aggregate investment is *irreversible*[6] *or* "largely irrevocable" despite the existence of organised stock exchange markets and other securities markets that are oriented to the provision of liquidity.
iv The stock exchange market is a rather *limited vehicle for delivering a correct valuation of investment plans*. Market participants are driven by *speculation* in the sense of anticipating average market valuations largely driven by mass psychology rather than by providing informed assessments of the long-run profitability of investment. The divergence between *social benefits* ("the defeat of the dark forces of time and ignorance") and *private incentives* (anticipating or speculating on the average valuation of the market) of "organised investment markets" suggests the limited usefulness of capital markets in a capitalist economy for a rational allocation of capital over time.

In Chapters 13 and 14 of Book IV, JMK makes a distinction between what he calls "the general theory of interest rate" versus the "classic theory of interest rate". In the first interest rates are determined in the money market by the equality between the *stock* supply and the *stock* demand for money. This is in contrast with interest rate determination in the savings and investment market – a flow equilibrium – as postulated by the classic tradition.

Keynes emphasised that there is a demand for money associated with the need to cope with uncertainty and enjoy the benefits of "being liquid", by holding monetary balances. In this context, the interest rate is *the price paid for holding liquid assets* – the foregone interest rate rate that would be earned if that amount of money were invested in yield-generating assets such as bonds, a stock or buying capital equipment that is put at work in a factory. In contrast, the classic theory of interest rates sees it as determined by the equilibrium between the flow of savings and the flow of investment. In this framework, the interest rate is interpreted as the *price of consumption today in terms of a sacrifice of future consumption*. Other interpretations view the interest rate as the "value of waiting" in the classic (pre-GT) theory.

Methodologically, Book IV represents new connections among money, investment and uncertainty underscoring:

i   *Fundamental uncertainty* is different from the notion of *risk* that attaches probabilities to a variety of events.
ii The critical role played by *investment and money in connecting the todays with the tomorrow* (through expectations).
iii The role of *money as an insurance* against uncertainty with the *interest rate being the premium (price) of buying an insurance position (acquiring liquidity)*.

Book V focuses on money wages, the employment function, and prices. In Chapter 19, a reduction of wages – seen as a cure for unemployment by the traditional approach – is analysed in terms of its impacts on the key variables of the macroeconomic model of the *General Theory*:

i   The propensity to consume
ii The marginal efficiency of capital
iii The preference for liquidity
iv The multiplier

These variables affect effective demand that determines the equilibrium level of output and employment. In the annex to Chapter 19, Pigou's *The Theory of Unemployment* is examined critically by Keynes showing that a reduction in real wages to clear the labour market will be of limited purpose in a world in which output and employment are determined by effective demand. Even the real wage reduction can be counterproductive if, for example, depresses consumption and effective demand. The marginal condition of the real wage equals the marginal productivity of labour derived from the production function no longer applies.

In Chapter 20, Keynes analyses the employment function as the inverse of the aggregate supply function – the Z-function – and connects employment with the level of effective demand, the length of the production period, the accrual of windfall profits and the effect of the multiplier. Chapter 21 studies the determination of the price level by the interplay between effective demand and aggregate supply. Here again Keynes notes the traditional separation between the theory of value and distribution on one side and the theory of money on another must be replaced by an approach that comprises two components: (i) a value theory at microeconomic level to determine *relative prices*, assuming a given level of output and resources for the economy as a whole and (ii) a macro theory of determination of output and employment according to the principle of effective demand. In this context, the price level is not determined by the quantity theory of money but by the equilibrium between aggregate demand and aggregate supply. In this context, there can be an *adjustment in both prices and output* following an increase in effective demand. The price effect will depend on the elasticity of the aggregate supply. A limit case would be an infinitely elastic aggregate supply (horizontal schedule) up to full employment and then a vertical supply schedule at full capacity. In this case, prices remain stable before full employment and if demand increases further then prices would rise but output would remain constant. However, JMK found more reasonable to assume a continuously upward-sloping supply schedule in which a rise in aggregate demand results in both quantity and price adjustments following, say , an increase in the supply of money.[7]

Book VI provides "Short Notes Suggested by the General Theory". Chapter 22 refers to the trade cycle and Chapter 23 refers to mercantilism, usury laws and under-consumption. JMK starts the discussion of Chapter 22 by highlighting that the GT is neither a theory that tries to explain the occurrence of cycles of regular duration and intensity nor a theory of the time sequence of booms and recessions. It is a book of equilibrium positions with some sketches of dynamics between those equilibrium positions. The novelty is the demonstration of *a stable equilibrium with involuntary unemployment and output below full capacity*. In that sense, and others, it departs from previous theories of the business cycle adopted by the Austrians (Hayek, Von Mises), Lionel Robbins and others. These theories are reviewed by G. Harberler in his *Prosperity and Recessions*, a book commissioned by the Economics Department of the League of Nations in the 1930s.

Attention is needed to clarify what are the main features of business cycle theory. In pre-Keynesian macroeconomics, a recession is often considered just as the natural sequence of a boom. If there were no boom, thus no recession would take place was the reasoning. In this context, the role of macro (monetary) policy should be to arrest (abort) a boom, basically by rising interest rates. That is the way to stabilise the economy and avoid a recession. Alternatively, there was a liquidation approach or do-nothing: policymakers just watch how the economic system purges itself of the excesses and inefficiencies of a phase of over-investment.[8]

In contrast, Keynes took as a *fact* the existence of slumps. Moreover, he generalised this as a normal situation of a capitalist economy independent if they are preceded by booms. The real question is what to do in the face of a slump, how to reduce unemployment, more than lamenting that policies did not abort a previous boom to start with.

Moreover, slumps are socially costly in terms of involuntary unemployment, compression of investment, individual anxiety and hardship. They entail a waste of valuable economic resources that remain idle. Under these conditions, the role of the policymakers must be to contain and mitigate these costs and help to surpass a slump. The exact origin of the slump cannot be easy to disentangle but once they occur, they can be protracted.

JMK underscored as an important cause (or perhaps symptom?) of a recession or slump in the *collapse* in the marginal efficiency of capital. Once this occurs, things can complicate further if there is an increase in the preference for liquidity (demand for money) that pushes up the interest rate bringing another recessive impulse.

Once a slump takes place the "restoration of confidence" – needed to reignite investment – is neither automatic nor instantaneous. The market is disoriented and affected by the vagaries of mass psychology and heterogeneous opinions among traders, businessmen, investors and the public, not to say the entrepreneur who is the producer. If confidence were a mechanical and predictable response function of certain stimulus – such as, for example, a cut in the interest rate – economic recoveries would be much easier to achieve.

In Keynes's own terms:

> It is the return of confidence, to speak in ordinary language, which is so insusceptible to control in an individualistic capitalist economy. This is the aspect of the slump which bankers and businessmen have been right in emphasising, and which the economists who have put their faith in a "purely monetary" remedy have underestimated.
>
> (GT, Ch. 22, p. 317)

A returning theme in Keynes is the behaviour, irregular and difficult to predict, of private investment:

> Any fluctuation in investment not offset by a corresponding change in the propensity to consume will, of course, result in a fluctuation in employment. Since, therefore, the volume of investment is subject to highly complex influences it is highly improbable that all fluctuations in investment itself or in the marginal efficiency of capital will be of a cyclical character.
>
> (GT, Ch. 22, p. 314)

The dynamics of the sequence of passing from a boom to a slump can be tricky as it involves a turn in expectations – intertwined with news and average opinions – from confidence to pessimism in the investment community – chiefly the players in the stock market – that leads to a selling-off of asset that depress their prices and negatively affect investment.

Keynes notes:

> I suggest that a more typical explanation of a crisis is not, primarily a rise in the interest rate, but a sudden collapse in the marginal efficiency of capital. The later stages of the boom are characterised by optimistic expectations as to the future yield of capital-goods sufficiently strong to offset its abundance or rising costs of production, and probably

a rise in interest rates also. It is of the nature of organised investment markets under the influence of purchasers largely ignorant of what they are buying and of speculators who are more concerned with forecasting the next of market sentiment than with a reasonable estimate of the future yield of capital-assets that, when disillusion falls upon an over-optimistic and overbought market, it should fall with sudden and even catastrophic force...liquidity preference ...does not increase until after a collapse in the marginal efficiency of capital. It is this, indeed, which renders the slump so intractable.

(GT, Ch. 22, p. 316)

To recover from a slump is often more complicated than just reducing the interest rate, argued JMK. It is necessary "to restore confidence" on the prospects of investment and the overall economy, a task that combines psychological demands as well as concrete policies.

JMK was sceptical that the private sector and markets alone will deliver by themselves the needed restoration of confidence that jump-start consumption, investment and the whole economy. He reviews alternatives to an investment-led recovery based on an increase in consumption based on the redistribution of incomes towards workers and the launching of employment programmes to counteract the depression of private investment. The following quotation shows his concerns on the limits of an automatic, private sector-led solution to pull the economy out of a slump:

In conditions of *laissez-faire* the avoidance of wide fluctuations in employment may, therefore, prove impossible without a far-reaching change in the psychology of investment markets such as there is no reason to expect. I conclude that the duty of ordering the current volume of investment cannot safely be left in private hands.

(GT, Ch. 22, p. 320)

Reactions to the *General Theory*

The GT, after its publication, became an instant success in terms of intense interest and attention by the profession of economists, the media and politicians. The trail record of immediate reactions is instructive. Initially, right after publication Keynes apparently intended to write a book entitled "Footnotes to the General Theory". However, the project came to a halt due to JMK's heart attack in May 1937 (*The Essential Keynes*, p. 263). Influential reviews of the GT were Jacob Viners' "Mr. Keynes and the Causes of Unemployment" published in the *Quarterly Journal of Economics*, November 1936 (Viner, 1936)[9]; Roy Harrod's "Mr. Keynes and Traditional Theory" in *Econometrica*, January 1937 (Harrod, 1937) and above all John Hicks's "Mr. Keynes and the "Classics": A Suggested Interpretation" appearing in *Econometrica*, April 1937 (Hicks, 1937). A few years later appeared Modigliani's "Liquidity Preference and the Theory of Interest and Money" published in *Econometrica* in January of 1944 containing a further treatment of the theory of preference for liquidity and integration in the analysis of the labour market, absent in Hicks (1937). Modigliani stressed the role of wage rigidity (and price stickiness) in driving the main results of the *General Theory*.

It is worth saying that while Hicks and Modigliani were, generally, sympathetic to the *General Theory*, Pigou and Harberler took a more critical stance. In the early 1940s, these two authors argued that the real balances effect invalidated the basic conclusions of the *General Theory*. The argument was that price deflation following a state of excess supply of goods and excess supply of labour in the economy would increase the real value of money, thereby inviting an increase in consumption and effective demand restoring full employment.

Additional perspectives to Keynes include Minsky (1975 [2008]) in which financial considerations are added. In fact, other followers of the master, some of them his former students who contributed to the making of the GT such as Joan Robinson, Richard Khan along with Nicholas Kaldor and others disagreed with the equilibrium interpretations of the *General Theory*. The polemic between the "hydraulic system" (Hicks and company) group and the "fundamentalist" branch (Robinson and followers) is still active (see *The Essential Keynes*).

Notes

1 Lange (1942).
2 Kalecki (1971), Feiwel (1975), and Rochon et al. (2022).
3 Luxemburg (1913 [2003]) and Lenin (1916 [1972]).
4 Both Franco Modigliani and Milton Friedman reformulated in the 1950s and 1960s the savings function. In Modigliani savings depends on life-cycle incomes and in Friedman consumption (and savings) depends on permanent incomes. Marglin (2021) offers criticisms of these two formulations and provides alternative theories of the consumption and saving function.
5 It is important to differentiate between the *natural* interest (a concept not used in the GT but used in the Treatise) and the *real* interest rate: both are defined in real terms, but the first is defined (Wicksell) as the rate consistent with the equality between savings and investment *at full employment* which is only considered as a special case in the *General Theory*.
6 See Pindyck and Solimano (1993).
7 In the quantity theory there is a proportional increase in money and prices assuming a constant income-velocity of money and a given level of output in the economy (a vertical aggregate supply).
8 See De Long (1990) for an exposition of the liquidation approach.
9 In Viner (1936) the author exposed his doubts on the meaning of involuntary unemployment in the GT, the distinction between nominal and real wage rigidity, the determination of interest rates by the preference for liquidity and other issues.

6 Interpreting "Keynes Macroeconomics" and Its Relevance for the 21st Century

JMK largely invented the field of modern macroeconomics, motivated on two levels.

The first one was analytical – to find a conceptual bridge between the theory of value and distribution (focused on relative prices, resource allocation and income distribution) and an explanation for aggregate variables, such as the price level, the level of output and employment. In other words, how to cross the bridge between two largely compartmentalised levels of analysis: the micro analysis and macro analysis in economic theory.

The second was a public policy-related motivation. In the 1920s, JMK wanted to stabilise the stagnant British economy at a high level of employment while maintaining price stability; in the 1930s, he wanted to overcome the Great Depression and reduce massive unemployment. JMK, the academic cum policy-maverick, started as a believer in the quantity theory of money (QTM) and Wicksell, which inspired the *Tract* and the *Treatise*; he then sharply departed from these frameworks in *The General Theory*.

For JMK, macroeconomics did not rest on extrapolating individual behaviour to aggregate (macro) behaviour, since doing so can lead to "fallacies of composition" and the capricious assumption of a strict connection between collective outcomes and individual motives. A well-known example of composition fallacy is the "paradox of thrift", in which the *attempt* to increase personal savings by the community may lead to a decline in aggregate *actual* savings. Macroeconomic outcomes are not a mechanical representation, at a larger scale, of individual motives and behaviour.

JMK uses economic identities such as the equality between total expenditures and real income at factor cost in the *Treatise* with its fundamental equations and in the *General Theory* with its definition of effective demand and its role in determining total output. In turn, JMK was careful to dismiss Say's law as a prediction that fails to hold in a monetary economy. He was also aware of the problems of causality and index numbers involved in the quantity theory of money.

DOI: 10.4324/9781003480785-6

Interpretations of the *General Theory* and Keynesian Economics

The publication of the GT and Keynesian economics gave rise to various interpretations of both their analytical content and their policy implications. The first break is between equilibrium/hydraulic/neoclassical synthesis and the fundamentalist interpretation. Then, we have the financial instability school (Minsky) and various political economy interpretations such as Kalecki's political theory of unemployment in modern capitalism.

Hicks' IS-LM Model

An early and perdurable equilibrium formalisation/interpretation of the GT was undertaken by Hicks (1937). The article introduced the famous model IS-LM, in which savings is a function of income, investment depends on the interest rate and the preference for liquidity (money demand) is a function of the interest rate and the level of income. Thus, a determined mathematical system comprising two equations and two unknowns seeks to capture the core analysis of the GT: the savings-equals-investment condition (goods-market equilibrium) and the money-market equilibrium in which the supply of money is equal to the demand for money. In turn, these two equations, in equilibrium, determine the two unknowns: the interest rate and the level of national income.

In this simplified representation, the price level is given exogenously, expectations have unitary elasticity, and the system does not explicitly incorporate a labour market. This simple (and neat) system allowed a rapid understanding of the GT, or at least parts of it (Chapter 12 and others are not much represented). The Hicks apparatus, flexible and sturdy, makes it possible to examine the effect of parametric changes in the supply of money, autonomous changes in consumption and investment, and increases in public spending. Although the IS-LM model became a valuable vehicle for teaching macroeconomics for decades, it was still an incomplete model of the macroeconomy in the sense that the model does not capture the labour market and aggregate supply along with an endogenous price level. In that sense, it can be interpreted more as a representation of the demand-driven economy in equilibrium.

Modigliani on Wage Rigidity and the Preference for Liquidity

Modigliani (1944) provides a more complete, albeit controversial, formal (algebraic) examination of the *General Theory*. His basic system of equations depicts (1) the money-market equilibrium, (2) the savings function and the investment function, (3) the savings-investment balance condition, (4) the determination of money income, (5) the production function, (6) the neoclassical demand for labour and (7) a dual specification of the supply of labour under wage rigidity and wage flexibility.

The paper also discusses the nature and stability of short-term and long-run macro-equilibrium, as well as alternative "closures" (specification of key macro relationships and their implication for the equilibrium of the system) representing the Keynesian and classical models. The differences between the two models centre around (i) the specification of the supply of labour, wage determination and the equilibrium of the labour market; and (ii) the demand for money. For Franco Modigliani, the GT assumes a fixed money wage at which there is an infinitely elastic supply of labour below full employment. Once full employment is reached, the supply is an upward function of the real wage, an endogenous (real) variable in the system.

JMK argued, based on his actual observation of labour-bargaining practices, that workers rarely accept a money-wage cut; thus, it is realistic to consider this variable as either a "predetermined" or a slow-adjusting variable. For Modigliani, "wage rigidity" is what generates a macro-equilibrium with unemployment, a main result of the GT: if wages and prices were fully flexible, there would be labour-market clearing and full employment.

The focus on wage rigidity/flexibility resembles the classic insistence that prices and wages clear the market. This follows a Walrasian general-equilibrium interpretation of Keynes, in line with authors such as Oskar Lange and Don Patinkin. The neoclassical synthesis attributed to Samuelson and Modigliani maintains that the GT equilibrium-with-unemployment result must be viewed as a short-run equilibrium. In the long run, when prices and wages are flexible, there will be full employment, and money is neutral. The classics are vindicated but only in the long run.

Summarising, Modigliani's (1944) article shows five important results:

i It is *wage rigidity* that renders possible the Keynesian result of an equilibrium with unemployment. This result is *not* due to the existence of a preference-for-liquidity function.

ii There are two "special cases" of macro-equilibrium in the GT worth considering: (a) the *liquidity trap*: a situation in which the demand for money is infinitely elastic at a certain, lower-bound, interest rate (a *horizontal* LM schedule in the relevant range); (b) the second special case is of an *interest rate insensitive demand for investment* schedule: a *vertical* IS schedule.

iii The macro-equilibrium defined in the GT as the simultaneous equality between savings and investment and money-market equilibrium will produce a full-employment equilibrium *only by chance*. No economic mechanism, under the assumptions of the book, guarantees that full employment is reached.

iv In a system in which the *demand for money does not depend on the interest rate* but only on real income (the Cambridge formulation of the QTM equation – that is, a vertical LM schedule in the interest-rate/income quadrant), the quantity of money affects only the price level and not the level of the real variables of the macro system; the real wage, the level of output, and the level of employment remain unchanged. This is, of course, a money-neutrality result.

v If there is *wage flexibility*, even if the demand for money depends on the interest rate (JMK's preference for liquidity), classic results will apply: money determines prices but not the real equilibrium variables of the system. This is the so-called classic dichotomy in which real variables are determined by real variables and nominal variables are determined by nominal variables (see Patinkin, 1965).

vi The *money supply and/or a change in the money wage* are the variables that can, in principle, be manipulated by policy and institutional reform to achieve full employment.

The Real Balance Effect

The "real balance effect" was advanced by authors generally unsympathetic to the unorthodox message of the *General Theory*, including Harberler (1952) and Pigou (1943, 1947). It is a potential way to restore full employment and escape the "Keynes trap" of a stable equilibrium with unemployment. The "*real balances effect*" refers to a change in the purchasing power of money held by individuals that is induced by an increase or decrease in the price level. The reasoning was explained earlier: if there is an excess supply of goods and an excess supply of labour (unemployment), prices and wages will fall, thereby raising the real value of money, thus increasing aggregate spending until full employment is reached.

The real balance effect is examined more fully, and clarified, by Patinkin (1965), an author who was generally appreciative of the key messages of the *General Theory* (although Patinkin, a student of Oskar Lange, was methodologically attached to a Walrasian–general equilibrium approach).

The *real balance effect* rests on at least two assumptions: (i) consumption depends on real wealth, not only on current income; (ii) the increase in real balances (cash and deposits) is not offset by an equal increase in the real value of debts (liabilities with the banking system).

As for the first assumption, it is true that while the GT posits that consumption is mainly a function of income, it certainly does include wealth among the list of factors (in Chapters 8 and 9) that also affect "the propensity to consume." It is unclear the extent to which JMK considered as practically relevant the real balance effect on consumption.

As for the debt effects and real balances effect of changing prices, Kalecki's (1944) response to Pigou's (1943) article "The Classic Stationary State" in *The Economic Journal* commented that if currency and deposits are backed exactly by loans and debts in the banking system, the fall in the price level will increase only the real stock of money backed by gold. If the stock of gold is small relative to the supply of money, then it will take a very large decline in the price level (and wages) to increase the real supply of money to attain full employment, dismissing the empirical importance of the real balance effect.[1]

Minsky's Financial Instability Hypothesis and Alternative Stabilisation Policies

Hyman Minsky provides another influential interpretation of JMK, emphasising business cycles, financial instability and unequal capitalism. His main books were:

- *John Maynard Keynes* (Minsky, 1975), Columbia University Press.
- *Can "It" Happen Again? Essays on Instability and Finance* (Minsky, 1982), M.E. Sharpe.
- *Stabilising An Unstable Economy* (Minsky, 1986), Mc-Graw Hill.

Minsky (1975) appreciated the role of uncertainty and instability in the formation of economic cycles and developed the theory of investment more fully, particularly its financing structure – a topic that was left relatively underdeveloped in the *General Theory*.

Minsky was against the equilibrium interpretation of JMK and repudiated the neoclassical synthesis that he believes played an important role in the turn to inflation and financial instability in the 1960s and 1970s in advanced capitalist economies, chiefly the United States, by promoting policies of fine-tuning of and an overly accommodative fiscal and monetary policy. In addition, Minsky (1975, 1986) was critical of policymakers who in the name of Keynesianism neglected GT's important insights about the actual behaviour of private investment (affected by uncertainty) and the true nature of financial markets (affected by fragility and speculation) in a capitalist economy. Part of this policy making "oversight" by the neoclassical synthesis of Keynes was due to an excessive faith prevailing in both academia and policy circles in the power of neoclassical optimisation, the efficiency of markets and a serious disregard for the pervasive presence of uncertainty. The *General Theory* was oriented precisely toward avoiding these flaws and biases in prevailing economic analysis. His followers apparently did not study the master's book carefully enough.

In "*Can It Happen Again?*" (Minsky, 1982), Minsky examines both the cash flows of enterprises and their balance sheet for an integral assessment of the financial health of the economy. He then proceeds to develop a taxonomy of the liability structure of investment of firms more fully, by including (a) hedge financing (cash flows safely finance both interest payments and capital amortisation), (b) speculative financing (cash flows are able to meet interest payments but not capital amortisation, which must be refinanced with new loans), and (c) Ponzi Financing (cash flows are unable to cover interest payments besides capital amortisations and are bound to return as growing, explosive levels of debt). Economies are financially stable only if the patterns of hedge financing dominate. A main point of Minsky is that macroeconomic analysis, as it evolved after the publication of the *General Theory*, systematically dismissed the importance of these financial considerations at the cost of disregarding the *endogenous* features of financial instability in a market economy.

In Minsky (1975, 1986), the author presents a formulation for monetary and fiscal policy that is an alternative to the post-World War II "Keynesian consensus." In particular, he notes the negative consequences for monetary stability of the confluence of Big Governments, the Big Bank (Federal Reserve), and Big Unions. This structure developed a monetary-fiscal accommodation bias (and a mentality of expecting bailouts) that was ultimately inflationary, since it created complacency in the corporate sector and the financial system and encouraged the adoption of speculative financing and Ponzi financing patterns that led to financial instability. These structural outcomes appeared more fully in the 1970s, 1980s, and 1990s. In addition, the welfare state, based on monetary transfers and social security, substituted for a policy of providing jobs directly in a full-employment direction.

JMK as an Economist of Inflation

JMK was not only the foremost "economist of depression", his more common ascription, but he was also an important "economist of inflation" to varying degrees. He had observed rapidly rising inflation since around 1913, a phenomenon that became even more severe in the first half of the 1920s and wanted to explain its causes, consequences and possible remedies.

In the *Tract* JMK showed (see chapter 3) how the demand for money fell during the high-inflationary episodes in Germany, Austria, and Russia, in the public's effort to avoid the inflation tax used to finance large fiscal budgets. The mirror effect of the decline in the demand for money was an increase in the velocity of circulation. Empirically, at very high rates of inflation, prices rise at a faster rate than money growth, with the difference being the increase in money velocity. The analysis in the *Tract* was influential for later analyses of inflation. They include Phillip Cagan's monetarist interpretation of explosive inflation (Cagan, 1956) and Milton Friedman's formulation of the "optimal quantity of money", stressing the loss in the indirect utility of the demand for money associated with the squeeze in the purchasing power of money taxed by inflation (Friedman, 1969).[2] For M. Friedman, the best book written by Maynard Keynes was the *Tract on Monetary Reform* (see Friedman, 1997).

In addition, JMK's analysis of European inflation in the 1910s and the 1920s – with its reliance on the fiscal deficit and its way of financing through money creation (inflation tax) and internal and external borrowing – influenced, years later, the techniques of financial programming linking money creation and fiscal budgets by the International Monetary Fund and its prescriptions for country monetary and fiscal programmes. In the 21st century, the IMF continues relying on financial programming techniques centred around the integration of monetary, fiscal, and balance of payments identities for its country programmes. IMF research uses Dynamic Stochastic General Equilibrium Models featuring "Keynesian rigidities" (wage stickiness; price rigidities) but the operational staff dealing with actual country programs still use flows of funds and financial programming models.

JMK's analysis stressed that explosive inflation would eventually affect the collection of the inflation tax depending on how the monetary base was shrinking, as people avoided holding money and shifted to real assets (property), jewelry, gold, paintings and more stable foreign currencies.

In both the *Tract* and the *Treatise, JMK* was critical of using "austerity policies" driven by high-interest rates to reduce wages and prices, essentially by inducing higher unemployment. He viewed this policy as economically and socially costly, besides politically inexpedient, particularly in a world of organised labour, active labour unions and wage resistance. His thoughts are very relevant for critically assessing today's austerity policies and shock treatment (see Mattei, 2022; Solimano, 2017).

He entertained the idea of national agreements among labour, capital associations, and governments to control inflationary pressures. These policies were indeed tried in different countries of Europe in the post–WWII period, and in Argentina, Brazil, and Israel during their high inflationary episodes in the 1980s, among other nations. Each attempted, with different degrees of success (or failure), to use *income-based* policy in which wage increases were coordinated with adjustments in the price of public utilities, profit margins, and exchange rates as a complement to fiscal adjustment. The objective was to reduce inflation without having to throw the economy into a protracted and costly path of recession and unemployment.

However, in the Neoliberal era, income-based policy to control inflation fell out of favour. Nowadays, the orthodox inflation-reduction method in which Central Banks use policies of higher interest rates, with its sequel of unemployment and stagnation, seems to be preferred by policy makers in different countries. Monetarism was adopted by Margaret Thatcher in the United Kingdom, by Ronald Reagan in the United States in the 1980s, and by General Pinochet in Chile in the 1970s, to cite notorious cases of inflation-reduction policies encompassing sharp reductions in the growth of money supply and fiscal deficits.[3] Of course, JMK was living in Great Britain's mature democracy, where discussions on economic austerity were not tainted by the recourse to authoritarianism. (However, the practices of economic policy under Fascism in Italy and Nazi rule in Germany were not that far from his home country.)

Another JMK inflation story (based on generalised excess demand) comes from his book *How to Pay for the War*, written in the early 1940s. The situation after the outbreak of WWII was different from the slump/stagnation and large surpluses of labour and physical capital of the early- to mid-1930s. In the early 1940s, there were *shortages* of goods and labour because a large volume of public demand for armaments was competing with private consumption and private investment in the economy. In this case, the situation exacted inflationary pressures for excess demand, or induced an "inflation gap", different from the lack of demand throughout most of the 1930s. Some goods were rationed, and the price of other goods rose, depressing real wages but increasing profits. "Profiteers" gained, while workers and recipients of fixed incomes (retired people and rentiers) suffered, creating unfair and undesired redistributions of income, which was not an encouraging situation for maintaining morale during wartime.

Keynes proposed that forced savings due to shortages and declining real wages be devoted to a system of deferred pay or compulsory savings that would be freely available at the end of the conflict. In this way a compression of consumption during wartime would become less arbitrary and transitory – more of a postponement of consumption over time rather than an irrevocable or permanent loss. JMK opposed wage increases to counteract price increases on the grounds that, because the economy was already at full employment, they would simply create a wage-price spiral; at the same time, he proposed a tax on excessive profits.

He also was *not* in favour of comprehensive rationing and preferred letting consumers decide what to do with their reduced available disposable income. In this case, inflation was the result of generalised excess demand. The calculations of *How to Pay for the War* were also a methodological contribution to the incipient use of economic planning techniques and demand management tools, since they entailed assessing potential output and employment under different scenarios, along with levels of aggregate demand in those conditions, and then measuring the gap between current and potential output.

Money and Finance through the *Tract, Treatise,* and the *General Theory*

In the *Tract*, JMK centres his analysis around the QTM, and the *Treatise* adds a Wicksellian mechanism of interest-rate determination. The two books are full of institutional details about the banking system and its connection with the money market. In contrast, there is very little mention of the banking sector in the *General Theory* and scant institutional detail.

The *Tract* and the *Treatise* delineated three main actors in the monetary-financial sector: the Central Bank (the Bank of England in Great Britain), the commercial banks that provide credit and manage the liquidity needs of their clients, and the public that maintains money as cash (notes and coins) and cheques held in current-account deposits in the commercial banks. The Bank of England had two important policy instruments at its disposal to regulate overall liquidity in the economy: (i) the discount rate, which affects the cost of acquiring advances in cash in exchange for financial instruments that commercial banks sell to the central bank; and (ii) the acquisition (or sale) of assets, such as Treasury bills, commercial bills, gold, and other securities.

The discount rate affects the cost of funding for the banks and therefore the stock of credit: a rise in the discount rate would lead to a lower supply of credit. Conversely, lowering the discount rate would encourage credit creation. At the same time, commercial banks had a policy (or a customary rule) of maintaining a certain proportion of their deposits in cash to stand ready to meet the liquidity claims of their clients. The cash-deposit ratio influences credit creation, since the more cash that is held in the central bank, the fewer the deposits that are available to back loans or support asset purchases by the commercial banks. In this framework, the interaction between the instruments of the central bank and the cash-deposits ratio of the banks played a fundamental role in regulating the price level and the state of production, sales, and employment in the economy.

The underlying theory of price-level determination and the business cycle is that the stock of money (currency notes, coins, and cheques) determines liquidity in conjunction with credit offered by the banks and is reflected by increases in the deposits of the banks. Credit issued by the banks, reflected in annotations in the deposit accounts of their clients, also creates liquidity and helps finance investment in fixed capital, working capital, and inventories. Credit also supports financing the acquisition of securities – bonds and shares – by the public and companies, in response to bull and bear positions associated with the public's state of confidence (optimism and pessimism).

The "credit cycle" plays a central role in inducing economic ups and downs, booms, and recessions. It is, implicitly, a largely financial theory of economic activity. In the GT, the principle of effective demand, with its components of consumption and investment, enters only as a determinant of economic activity (it was not part of the analytical apparatus of either the TMR or the *Treatise*).

The determination of the market interest rate in the *Treatise* takes place in the credit market, along the lines of Knut Wicksell's loanable-funds market formulation. His construction is a specification of flows of savings (supply of funds) and investment (demand for funds) complemented by the distinction between the market interest rate and the natural interest rate. The *Treatise* seeks to integrate Wicksell with the QTM in long-run equilibrium. The discrepancies between the market interest rate and the natural rates constitute an indicator to the central bank to adjust the discount rate to regulate the flow of credit in the economy. If investment exceeds savings, it means the market interest rate is below the natural rate, thus requiring an increase in the discount rate. Conversely, an excess of savings over investment calls for lowering the discount rate.

In the GT, JMK discards both the QTM and Wicksell's loanable-funds formulation.

The interest rate is no longer the mechanism that equilibrates the supply of savings with the demand for investment. Furthermore, the distinction between the market interest rate and the natural rate is no longer necessary. In the GT the interest rate equilibrates the supply of money and the demand for money (or the demand for bonds and the supply of bonds). Because the price of bonds is the present discounted value of the annuities at a certain interest rate, the changes in bond prices/interest rates equilibrate both the bond market and the money market.

The theory of the preference for liquidity in the GT replaces the loanable-funds story of the *Treatise*. Money, the most liquid asset, is held for motives introduced in the GT: transaction, precaution, and speculation. The interest rate represents the opportunity cost of holding money and must be balanced with the various conveniences of holding money and "being liquid."

In the GT, JMK reviews various theories of interest-rate determination associated with the value of waiting and the price of current consumption vis-a-vis future consumption and contrasts them with his new theory of interest as the price of liquidity. People need a liquid asset to undertake retail transactions, to face unexpected contingencies and to take advantage of transitory undervalued assets that, when misalignments are corrected, will generate windfall capital gains to security holders. Savers (widows, orphans, and rentiers) matter less in driving interest-rate movements than are speculators playing the stock and bond markets. JMK's active, real-world experience in financial markets and deals suggested to him that relative supply and demand positions for securities are what drive the market. Asset prices and interest rates jump in response to news and changes in sentiment and expectations in financial markets.

The shift of view about the focal point on financial markets is evident between the *Treatise* and the *General Theory*. In the *Treatise* Keynes focused on bank credit, cash ratios, and central bank manipulations of liquidity and discount rates. The indicator of whether interest rates were "correct" – or required adjustment – centred on the differences between market and natural rates of interest. An upward pressure in prices can indicate an excess of investment over savings that requires an increase in the market interest rate.

In the *General Theory*, the focus is on the money market and the bond market, and their rapid adjustments to surrounding real and financial conditions. In turn, JMK expresses his distrust of the stock market as an ultimately dysfunctional mechanism – albeit one hard to replace – in which valuations for investment reflect more subjective expectations and herd behaviour than they do rational long-term evaluations of the future productivity of physical capital.

Still, one can see some elements of continuity between the *Treatise* and the *General Theory* regarding the specification of the demand for money. In the *Treatise* JMK terms the proportion of time-deposit/checking accounts that are used for current transactions by the public and business firms (wage payments and input expenses) as "industrial circulation." In turn, he labels the proportion of deposits used to acquire bonds and stocks as "financial circulation."

In the *General Theory* JMK separates the demand for money into two broad components: a first component that corresponds to the demand for money for transaction purposes (and precaution), generally depending on the level of income; and a second component, the demand for money for "speculation" purposes, depending on the interest rate. This second component is the demand for money held for the purpose of buying stocks and bonds. The speculative demand for money in the GT strongly resembles the financial circulation of the *Treatise*. In turn, the demand for money for transaction purposes amounts, roughly, to the demand for money for "industrial circulation."

How to Get Full Employment? The Limits of Monetary Expansion and Political Economy Constraints on Fiscal Policies

JMK was sceptical that monetary policy alone could be effective at overcoming a slump if the interest rate is very low and the demand for money is infinitely elastic (liquidity trap). In this case, the extra money injected into the economy will be absorbed entirely by the public: the additional money will have little or no impact on the interest rate and investment in a liquidity trap. In addition, if the marginal efficiency of capital (MEC) collapses, the revival of investment requires that "animal spirits" reawaken and pull investment. A simple change in the interest rate that does not turn around expectations and restore optimism in the business community will not do the trick (of reviving investment). In the conditions of a profound slump that has shattered expectations and created a pessimistic assessment of the future state of the economy, a programme of public investment to build roads, highways, schools and hospitals, water and sanitation facilities, and telecommunication networks is a better alternative. This was the position of JMK (writing with Henderson) to create employment and break a long stagnation trap in the pamphlet "Can Lloyd George Do It?" in support of the candidate of the Liberal Party in the general elections of 1929. In this case, with a programme of public investment, the injection of purchasing power in the economy is direct (monetary policy acts indirectly), and the effect on effective demand is amplified further by the operation of the multiplier, whose magnitude is dependent on the marginal propensity to consume. This is the main rationale for using fiscal policy, as JMK explains in the *General Theory*.

Nowadays, debates between the convenience of monetary and fiscal policy for stimulating the economy after a recessionary shock continue. JMK's influence endures, despite the retreat of Keynesian economics in academia and policy circles starting in the 1970s. The reality is that fiscal tools are still used when big slumps hit the economy: this was the case with the global financial crisis of 2008–2009 and the COVID crisis of 2020–2021. On monetary policy, the central banks of advanced economies have made a selected return to the concept of the natural interest rate advanced by Wicksell – but now in terms of a "neutral interest rate", defined as a rate that produces neither acceleration or deceleration of inflation. This is, of course, an *unobserved* variable, and proxy estimates using econometric methods are not always fully convincing. For the Keynes of the GT, the relevant variable was the market interest rate (short- and long-term rates).

Fiscal policy as a tool to get full employment has always been subject to a degree of hostility by the defenders of the "free market" and the alleged superiority of the private sector. The classic school that faced Keynes argued that state intervention in the economy would always make things worse as it would subtract financial and physical resources that otherwise could be utilised by the private sector in more productive ways. Of course, the stagnation of the 1920s in the United Kingdom and then the great depression of the 1930s argued in favour of Keynes that the alternative of state no intervention in the economy is that resources would remain idle (unemployed labour and unused productive capacity in firms) rather than being automatically used in a productive way by the private sector. The "crowding-out" argument – each point of public investment or public consumption would displace an x amount of private investment and/or private consumption – rests on the impact of public spending on interest rates making more expensive credit for the private sector (and the government). Another mechanism is the expectation of future taxes inferred by the public when they see the government has increased public spending (for example when financed by public debt) and sooner or later will have to balance the fiscal budget.

Another argument coming from progressive economists such as Michael Kalecki points out in his article "Political Aspects of Full Employment" written in 1943 (see Kalecki, 1971, chapter 12) in which it is argued that in a capitalist economy, the ruling class will value even more than avoiding business cycles and having full employment, the control of the productive process – chiefly the labour process (with capital setting wages and working conditions) by the owners of capital that are also politically influential. In this condition, it is highly *unlikely* that governments will follow a permanent policy of full employment that increases the bargaining power of workers as they know they will not face the disciplinary mechanism of becoming unemployed. Hyman Minsky, among others, has argued (see Minsky, 1975, chapter 8) that the recourse to military spending and/or the actual waging of war has been a widely used method to stimulate the economy and advance to full employment (Keynes was against military stimulus). This was the case in Germany and Japan in the second half of the 1930s, in several belligerent countries during World War II and in the post-war period: the Korean War, the Vietnam War, the Iraq War and other conflicts in the 21st century.

Keynesian macroeconomics, we believe, keeps vitality and relevance for today's macroeconomic challenges around the world. The return of inflation after COVID brings about the insights and analysis of JMK's *Tract* and the *Treatise*. The methods and insights of *How to Pay for the War* are still relevant for countries experiencing armed conflicts. Macroeconomic fluctuations are present in most economies, and the lessons of the GT and other writings are relevant. At the more theoretical level the search for micro-foundations and maximisation underpinning macro-relations that dominated macroeconomics since the 1970s are being complemented by the incorporation of behavioural economics and the search for new frameworks and paradigms that are more realistic of actual human behaviour than pure maximisation.

Still, the legacy of the multidimensional John Maynard Keynes – the academic, the policy advisor, the statesman, the thinker, the humanist – seems to be well alive.

Notes

1 In modern language, only "outside money" – that is, money that is net wealth – counts for the real balance effect to operate. If money has a counterpart of debt, the effect of the price level on real balances will be small. Remember, this is a net-wealth effect, so liabilities must be deducted from assets; it is *net* wealth that matters for a net effect of the price level.

2 In the 1970s, reviews by Franco Modigliani and Stanley Fischer of the costs of inflation and their emphasis on menu costs and transaction costs reflected JMK's analysis in the *Tract*.

3 In Chile in the 1970s, it took protracted unemployment for several years to start the convergence to one-digit inflation after a policy of shock treatment was promoted by Milton Friedman in his visit to Santiago in 1975. On that occasion Friedman delivered to General Pinochet a detailed report on how Chile could stabilise the economy by cutting public spending, increasing taxes, slowing monetary growth, and repressing wages. His former students, known as the "Chicago Boys", were reaching ministerial positions in the Pinochet regime, and worked hard to adopt the policies of their professor in the second half of the 1970s – at a high social cost. Of course, these policies could be implemented in Chile as trade-union activity was completely curtailed and labour leaders were actively persecuted by the military (see Solimano, 2012; Solimano and Zapata-Roman, 2024).

References

Amadeo, E.J. (1989) *Keynes's Principle of Effective Demand.* Edward Elgar, Aldershot Hants, and Brookfield, Vermont.

Barsky, R.B. and L.H. Summers (1988) "The Gibson Paradox and the Gold Standard," *The Journal of Political Economy* 96(3):528–550.

Bresciani-Turroni, C. (1937) *The Economics of Inflation: A Study of Currency Depreciation in Post-War Germany, 1914–1923.* Oxfordshire, Routledge.

Brown, C.E. (1940) "Fiscal Policies in the 1930s: A Reappraisal," *American Economic Review* 46: December, 857–879.

Cagan, P. (1956) "The Monetary Dynamics of Hyperinflation," M. Friedman (ed). *Studies in the Quantity Theory of Money.* Chicago, IL: University of Chicago Press.

Clarke, P. (2009) *Keynes. The Twentieth Century's Most Influential Economist.* London, Berlin and New York: Bloomsbury.

Crotty, J. (2019) *Keynes against Capitalism. His Economic Case for Liberal Socialism.* London and New York: Routledge, Taylor & Francis.

De Long, B. (1990) "Liquidation Cycles: Old Fashioned Real Business Cycle Theory and the Great Depression". NBER Working Paper 3546. National Bureau of Economic Research.

Dornbusch, R. and S. Fischer (1986) "Stopping Hyperinflations Past and Present," *Weltwirtschaftliches Archiv* 122(1):1–47.

Edwards, S. (2018) *American Default. The Untold Story of FDR, the Supreme Court and the Battle over Gold.* Princeton: Princeton University Press.

Eichengreen, B. (1992) *Golden Fetters: The Gold Standard and the Great Depression.* Oxford: Oxford University Press.

Eloranta, J. (2007) "From the Great Illusion to the Great War: Military Spending Behaviour of the Great Powers, 1870–1913," *European Review of Economic History* 11(2):255–283.

———— (2013) "World War I," R. Parker and R. Whales (eds). *Handbook of Major Events in Economic History.* London and New York: Routledge, Francis & Taylor Group.

Feinstein, C., P. Temin and G. Tonolio (2008) *The World Economy between the Wars.* New York and Oxford: Oxford University Press.

Feiwel, G.R. (1975) *The Intellectual Capital of Michal Kalecki. A Study in Economic Theory and Policy.* Knoxville: University of Tennessee Press.

Fetter, F.W. (1977) "Lenin, Keynes and Inflation," *Economica,* 173: February, Wiley, 77–80.

Fisher, I. (1911) *The Purchasing Power of Money: Its Determination in Relation to Credit, Interest and Crises.* New York: Macmillan.

———— (1930) *The Theory of Interest. As Determined by Impatience to Spend Income and Opportunity to Invest It*. New York: Macmillan.

Frieden, J.A. (2007) *Global Capitalism: Its Fall and Rise in the Twentieth Century*. New York: W.W. Norton & Company.

Friedman, M. (1969) *The Quantity Theory of Money and Other Essays*. Chicago, IL: Aldine.

———— (1997) "John Maynard Keynes" in *Federal Reserve Bank of Richmond Economic Quarterly*, vol. 83/2, Spring.

Graham, F.D. (1930) *Exchange, Prices, and Production in Hyper-Inflation: Germany, 1920–1923* (Vol. 1). Auburn: Ludwig von Mises Institute.

Gramsci, A. (1920 [1968]) "Soviets in Italy. Workers Democracy," reprinted in *The New Left Review* I(51): September/October, 28–58.

Hansen, A. (1932) "A Fundamental Error in Keynes's Treatise on Money," *American Economic Review* 22(3): September, 462. Published by the American Economic Association.

Harberler, G. (1952) "The Pigou Effect Once More," *Journal of Political Economy* LX:240–246.

Harrod, R. (1937) "Mr. Keynes and Traditional Theory," *Econometrica 5*, January, 74–86.

———— (1951) *The Life of John Maynard Keynes*. New York and London: W.W. Norton & Co.

Hatton, T.J. and J.G. Williamson (2005) *Global Migration and the World Economy. Two Centuries of Policy and Performance*. Cambridge: MIT Press.

Hayek, F.A. (1931) "Reflections on the Pure Theory of Money of Mr. J.M. Keynes," *Economica* 33: August, 270–295.

———— (1932) "Reflections on the Pure Theory of Money of Mr. J.M. Keynes (continued)," *Economica* 35:22–44.

Hicks, J. (1937) "Mr. Keynes and the "Classics": A Suggested Interpretation," *Econometrica*, April, 147–59.

Humphrey, T.M. (1996) "The Early History of the Box Diagram," *Federal Reserve Bank of Richmond Economic Quarterly* 82/1: Winter, 37–75.

James, H. (2002) *The End of Globalization. Lessons from the Great Depression*. Cambridge, MA: Harvard University Press.

Kahn, R.F. (1984) *The Making of Keynes' General Theory*. Raffaele Mattioli Lectures. Cambridge: Cambridge University Press.

Kalecki, M. (1944) "Professor Pigou on the "Classical Stationary State" a Comment," *The Economic Journal* 54(213):131–132.

———— (1971) *Selected Essays on the Dynamics of the Capitalist Economy 1933–1970*. Cambridge: Cambridge University Press.

Katzenellebaum, S. (1925) *Russian Currency and Banking*. London: Orchard House.

Keynes, J.M. (2013 [1913]) *Indian Currency and Reform*, the Collected Writings of John Maynard Keynes (Vol. I). Cambridge: Cambridge University Press.

———— (1971 [1920]) *The Economic Consequences of Peace*. New York: Penguin Books.

———— (2000 [1923]) *A Tract on Monetary Reform*. New York: Prometheus Books, Great Minds Series.

———— (2011 [1930]) *A Treatise on Money* (Vols. I and II). New York: Martino Publishing CT, Harcout Brace and Company.

———— (1931) "The Pure Theory of Money. A Reply to Dr. Hayek," *Economica* 34: November, 387–397.

───── (1964 [1936]) *The General Theory of Employment, Interest and Money.* San Diego, CA, New York and London: A Harvest/HBJ Book, Harcout, Brace, Jovanovich Publishers.

Kindleberger, Ch. (2013 [1973]) *The World in Depression 1929–1939.* Oakland: University of California Press.

Lange, O. (1942) Say's law: A restatement and criticism, *Studies in Mathematical Economics and Econometrics, in Memory of Henry Schultz,* edited by O. Lange, F. McIntyre, and T. O. Yntema (pp. 49–68), Chicago: University of Chicago Press.

Leijonhufvud, A. (1968) *On Keynesian Economics and the Economics of Keynes. A Study in Monetary Theory.* London and Toronto: Oxford University Press.

Lenin, V.I. (1972 [1916]) *Imperialism: The Highest Stage of Capitalism.* New York: International Publishers.

Luxemburg, R. (2003 [1913]) *The Accumulation of Capital.* London and New York: Routledge Classics.

Maddison, A. (2013) *The Maddison Project.* http://www.ggdc.net/maddison/maddison-proyect/home.htm, 2013 version.

Marglin, S.A. (2021) *Raising Keynes. A Twenty-First Century General Theory.* Cambridge, MA and London: Harvard University Press.

Marshall, A. (1890 [1961]) *Principles of Economics,* 1st ed. London: Macmillan. Ninth Edition for the Royal Economic Society, 1961.

Mattei, C.E. (2022) *The Capital Order. How Economists Invented Austerity and Paved the Way to Fascism.* Chicago, IL and London: The Chicago University Press.

Minsky, H.P. (1975 [2008]) *John Maynard Keynes.* New York: Mc Graw Hill.

Modigliani, F. (1944) "Liquidity Preference and the Theory of Interest and Money," *Econometrica* XII: January, 45–88.

Moggridge, D.E. (1992) *Maynard Keynes. An Economist's Biography.* London and New York: Routledge, Taylor & Francis Group.

Myrdal, G. (1939 [1965]) *Monetary Equilibrium,* reprints of Economic Classics, Augustus, M. Kelley. New York: Bookseller.

Nenovsky, N. (2015) The Soviets Monetary Experience (1917–1924) through the Perspective of the Discussion on Unity and Diversity of Money. CRIISEA, University of Picardie Jules Verne, France, RUDN, Russia.

Palairet, M. (2000) *The Four Ends of the Greek Hyperinflation of 1941–1946.* Copenhagen: Museum Tusculanum Press, University of Copenhagen.

Patinkin, D. (1948) "Price Flexibility and Full Employment," *The American Economic Review* 38(4):543–564.

───── (1965) *Money, Interest and Prices. An Integration of Monetary and Value Theory,* 2nd ed. New York: Harper & Row, Publishers.

───── (1982) *Anticipations of the General Theory? And Other Essays.* Chicago, IL: The University of Chicago Press.

Pigou, A.C. (1943) "The Classic Stationary State," *Economic Journal* 53(212):343–351.

───── (1947) "Economic Progress in a Stable Environment," *Economica* XIV, 55, August, Wiley, 180–188.

Pindyck, R. and A. Solimano (1993) "Economic Instability and Aggregate Investment," O. Blanchard and S. Fischer (eds). *NBER Macroeconomic Annual.* Cambridge, MA: The MIT Press.

Polanyi, K. (1944) *The Great Transformation. Economic and Political Origins of Our Time.* New York: Rinehart.

Preobrazhensky, E. (1926) "On Primary Socialist Accumulation," reprinted and translated in *Foundations of Soviet Strategies of Economic Growth, Selected Essays, 1924–1930*, edited by N. Spulber, Bloomington: Indiana University Press, 1964.

Ritschl, A. (2005) "The Pity of Peace: Germany's Economy at War, 1914–1918 and Beyond," Chapter 2, S. Broadberry and M. Harrison (eds). *The Economics of World War I*. Cambridge: Cambridge University Press.

Robertson, D.H. (1926) *Banking Policy and the Price Level. An Essay in the Theory of the Trade Cycle*. London: P.S. King & Son.

Rochon, L.-P., M. Czachor and G.R. Bachurewicz, editors (2022) *Kalecki and Kaleckian Economics. Understanding the Economics of Michal Kalecki and His Legacy after 50 Years*. London and New York: Routledge, Taylor & Francis Group.

Rockoff, H. (2005) "Until It Is Over, Over There: The US Economy in WWI," Chapter 10, S. Broadberry and M. Harrison (eds). *The Economics of World War I*. Cambridge: Cambridge University Press.

Romer, C.D. (1990) "The Great Crash and the Onset of the Great Depression," *The Quarterly Journal of Economics* 105(3): August, 597–624.

——— (1992) "What Ended the Great Depression?" *The Journal of Economic History* 52(4): December, 757–784.

Sargent, T.J. (1982) "The Ends of Four Big Inflations," *Inflation: Causes and Effects*. Chicago, University of Chicago Press, pp. 41–98.

Schumpeter, J.A. (1954) *A History of Economic Analysis*. New York: Oxford University Press.

Skidelsky, R. (1992) *John Maynard Keynes. Vol. II. The Economist as Savior, 1920–1937, a Biography*. London: Allen Lane, The Penguin Press.

——— (2000) *John Maynard Keynes. Vol. III. Fighting For Freedom, 1937–1946, a Biography*. London: Viking, The Penguin Group.

——— (2015) *John Maynard Keynes. The Essential Keynes*. London: Penguin Books, Classics.

Solimano, A. (1990) "Inflation and the Costs of Stabilization: Country Experience, Conceptual Issues and Policy Lessons," *The World Bank Research Observer* 5(2), July:176–185.

——— (1991) "The Economies of Central and Eastern Europe: An Historical and International Perspective," V. Corbo, F. Coricelli and J. Bossak (eds). *Reforming Central and Eastern European Economies. Initial Results and Challenges*. A World Bank Symposium, Washington DC.

——— (2012) *Chile and the Neoliberal Trap. The Post-Pinochet Era*. Cambridge and New York: Cambridge University Press.

——— (2017) *Global Capitalism in Disarray, Inequality, Debt and Austerity*. Oxford and New York: Oxford University Press.

——— (2020) *A History of Big Recessions in the Long Twentieth Century*. Cambridge and New York: Cambridge University Press.

——— (2022) *Economic and Political Democracy in Complex Times*. London and New York: Routledge, Francis & Taylor Group.

Solimano, A. and G. Zapata-Roman (2024) *Chilean Economic Development under Neoliberalism: Structural Transformation, High Inequality and Environmental Fragility, Series Elements in Development*. Cambridge and New York: Cambridge University Press.

Taylor, L. (2010) *Maynard's Revenge. The Collapse of Free Market Macroeconomics.* Cambridge, MA and London: Harvard University Press.

Twoney, M.J. (1983) "The Great Depression in Latin America; A Macro Analysis," *Explorations in Economic History* 20:221–247.

Végh, C.A. (1992) "Stopping High Inflation: An Analytical Overview," *IMF Staff Papers* 39(3):626–695.

Viner, J. (1936) "Mr. Keynes and the Causes of Unemployment," The *Quarterly Journal of Economics*, November, 147–67.

Wicksell. K. (1911 [1936, English edition]) *Interest and Prices: A Study of the Causes Regulating the Value of Money.* London: Macmillan.

Index

Note: Page numbers followed by "n" denote endnotes.

accommodative monetary policy 10, 24, 37, 49, 69
aggregate demand 31, 82, 83, 88, 94, 105
aggregate employment 12, 87
aggregate investment 92
aggregate supply 93, 94, 99
Amadeo, E.J. 75
American financing 27–30
Appreciation and Interest (Fisher) 41
Arian supremacy 5
Arrow's impossibility theorem 15n1
Aster Revolution 21
Australia 16, 29, 30, 52
Austria 2, 10, 19, 23, 29, 30, 33, 37, 44, 45, 55
Austro-Hungarian empire 17–19, 35n8

bank credit 59, 65, 107
banking crises 29–30
Banking Policy and the Price Level (Robertson) 58
banking system 6, 8, 11, 53, 56–58, 65, 66, 68, 77, 78, 84, 101, 102
bank money 61, 65, 67, 72, 77, 78
bank rate 49, 55, 66, 67, 69, 77
barter economy 60, 81, 83
Bolshevik revolution 20
bond market 83, 107
Bresciani-Turroni, C. 23, 24, 35n14
Britain 17, 19
British economy 26, 57
Brown, Cary 32
Bukharin, Nicolas 22

Cambridge Equation 47
"Can It Happen Again?" (Minsky) 102

capital 13, 14, 16, 40, 46, 65, 68, 71, 72, 78, 85, 87, 90, 95, 96; formation 13, 14, 40, 84; investments 71, 77
capitalism 4, 8, 23, 46, 59, 71
capitalist economy 3, 13, 14, 71, 85, 87, 92, 94, 102, 109
The Carthaginian Peace or the Economic Consequences of Mr. Keynes (Mantoux) 28
cash 27, 32, 47–49, 53, 54, 56, 101, 106; deposits 65, 68, 69, 72, 77, 78; flows 102, 103
Cassel, Gustav 10, 50
cheques 47–49, 54, 106
"Chicago Boys" 110n3
classic gold 25, 26, 37, 50, 52, 56
The Collected Writings of John Maynard Keynes 3, 6
commercial banks 10, 19, 21, 30, 36, 47–49, 53, 54, 67, 73, 106
commodity inflation 11, 66
compensated dollar plan 42
competition 17, 74, 86
Conference of Genoa of 1922 20
consumer goods price 11
consumption 11–13, 58, 59, 61, 62, 87, 88, 90, 92, 96, 97, 101, 105; goods 47, 48, 56, 57, 61–64, 68
contracts 36, 38, 45–47, 51
credit 31, 48, 49, 53–56, 58, 65–67, 71, 77, 78, 106; cycle 48, 59, 69, 71, 72, 75, 78, 106
currency 24–27, 30, 33, 37, 38, 43–45, 50, 51, 53, 54; notes 43, 44, 106
current investment 90

Dawes Plan in 1924 27, 28, 34
deflation 10, 37, 38, 40–42, 45, 51, 55, 66, 90
deposits 29, 31, 47, 48, 53, 54, 61, 64, 68, 77, 101, 102, 106, 108
depression 2, 6, 8, 14, 21, 28–31, 33, 73, 80, 82
devaluation 46, 51
discount rate 10, 48, 56, 90, 106, 107
distinction 11, 12, 59, 68, 75, 77, 92, 106, 107
domestic inflation 52, 76
domestic price deflation 30
dual price theory cost 11

Econometrica 96, 97
economic activity, effects 19
The Economic Consequences of Mr. Churchill (Keynes) 26
The Economic Consequences of Peace (Keynes) 2, 5
economic growth 10, 32–34, 40, 71
economic policies 32, 34, 105
economic policy objectives 76–77
Economics of Welfare (Pigou) 9
economic system 14, 37, 45, 55, 77
economic theories 3, 98
economists 1, 71, 73, 84, 86, 87, 95, 96
Edgeworth, Francis Y. 9
effective demand 7, 8, 12–15, 19, 82–87, 93, 97
Eichengreen, B. 35n20
employment 12–14, 31, 60, 75, 76, 80–82, 85–88, 93, 94, 97, 100, 101, 109; creation 69, 80; determination 10, 12; equilibrium 14, 60, 85, 100; function 93
England 4, 10, 14, 16, 25, 26, 48, 53, 54, 70, 73, 106
equilibrium 9, 13, 14, 57, 58, 60, 63–65, 75, 83, 92, 93, 99, 100
Europe 2, 4, 6, 20, 21, 27–29, 37–40, 52, 55; recovery in 33–34
European revolutions 17
excess demand 8, 10, 58, 83, 105
exchange economy 60, 81
exchange rate 5, 8, 21, 24, 27, 30–32, 36, 37, 50–52, 54, 56; determination 10, 47–49, 55
expected inflation 73, 90
explosive inflation 10, 20, 23, 45, 104

February Revolution in 1917 21
finance 2–4, 39, 53, 54, 56, 65, 68–70, 77, 78, 102, 103
financial circulation 8, 77, 108
financial instability 19, 102, 103
financial markets 6, 69, 102, 107
fiscal policies 13–15, 32, 54, 103, 108, 109; political economy constraints on 108–110
Fischer, Stanley 110n2
Fisher, Irving 41–43, 47, 54, 58, 73, 90
forced savings 60, 75, 76, 105; mechanism 75, 76
foreign currency 24, 25, 50, 51, 54
foreign direct investment 16, 58
foreign exchanges 36–56
foreign goods 37, 50, 56, 57
France 4, 16, 17, 19, 23, 26, 27, 33, 34, 38, 46
Friedman, Milton 49, 56, 110n3
full employment 108–110

The General Theory of Employment, Interest and Money (GT) (Keynes) 6, 8, 10, 12–14, 57, 80–97, 107, 108; interpretations 99; reactions 96–97
German economy 17, 27, 28, 34
German hyperinflation 35n14
Germany 1, 2, 16, 18–20, 23, 27–30, 33, 34, 38, 45
Gibson paradox 73
globalisation 16, 17
Graham, F.D. 23, 24, 35n14
Gramsci, Antonio 21
Great Depression 29, 30, 98
The Great Transformation (Polanyi) 17

Hicks, J. 97, 99
Hicks' IS-LM model 99
high rates of inflation 45, 103
A History of Economic Analysis (Schumpeter) 88
home investment 16, 81
How to Pay for the War (Keynes) 2, 105
Hungarian Soviet Revolution 21
Hungary 2, 18, 20, 21, 23, 35n11, 37
hyperinflation 2, 20, 23, 44, 45, 55
hyperinflation, Central Europe 23; case of Germany 23–24; currencies and inflation, Soviet Russia 24–25; gold standard and stagnation, Britain 25–27

income 10–13, 36–38, 42, 47, 61, 75, 88, 89, 99, 104; deposits 68, 77; inflation 11, 66, 70, 71
Indian Currency and Finance (Keynes) 4
industrial circulation 8, 11, 108
inflation 10, 19, 24, 36, 38–42, 44–46, 55, 103, 104; evil of 36–56; rate 38, 42; tax 10, 23, 37, 43–47, 49, 55, 56, 103, 104
Interest and Prices: A Study of the Causes Regulating the Value of Money (Wicksell) 58
interest rates 12–14, 66, 70, 71, 73, 77, 78, 85, 88, 92, 95, 96, 99, 100, 107, 108
international trade 23, 50, 51
investment 11–13, 58, 59, 61, 63–67, 69–72, 74, 78, 88, 90–92, 95, 96; community 59, 71; fluctuations in 79, 95; function 71, 84, 90; goods 11, 12, 78; markets 92, 96
involuntary unemployment 87
Italy 19

John Maynard Keynes (JMK) 25; advisor 2; British Treasury and 2; dysfunctional economy 2; *The Economic Consequences of Mr. Churchill* 26; *The Economic Consequences of Peace* 5, 28, 29; economic plans 3; economist of inflation 103–105; *The General Theory of Employment, Interest, and Money* (GT) 6, 8, 10, 12–14, 57, 80–97; gold standard, suspension of 1; *How to Pay for the War* 2, 105; *Indian Currency and Finance* 4; literature on (writings) 3–4; macroeconomics 7–15, 98–110; reassessment of quantity theory (QT) 67–68; talents and interests 4–7; *A Tract on Monetary Reform* (TMR) 8, 10, 12, 19, 36–56; *A Treatise on Money* (TM) 6, 8, 10–13; *The Treatise on Probability* 5

Kaldor, Nicholas 59
Kalecki, M. 7, 31, 87, 101
Keynes, John Maynard *see* John Maynard Keynes

Keynes-Olivera-Tanzi effect 39
Kindleberger, Ch. 35n17

labour market 9, 83, 86, 93, 97, 99, 100
liquidity: preference for 99–101
local currency 50, 51, 54
Luxemburg, Rosa 87

Maddison, A. 35n13
The Manchester Guardian Commercial 2, 36
Mantoux, Etienne 28
marginal efficiency of capital (MEC) 90, 108
market economy 25, 56, 70, 103
market equilibrium 99, 100
market interest rate 11, 12, 59, 60, 66, 67, 69, 72, 78, 106, 107, 109
Marshall, Alfred 9, 74
Marshallian equilibrium 74–76
Marx, Karl 87
military spending 18, 34, 109; rise and fall in 18
Minsky, H.P. 102, 103; alternative stabilisation policies 102–103; financial instability hypothesis 102–103
Modigliani, F. 99, 100, 110n2; on wage rigidity 99–101
monetarism 41, 104
monetary authorities 37, 49, 54, 56, 69, 78
monetary expansion: limits of 108–110
monetary factors 69–72
monetary policy 5, 13, 14, 36, 37, 49, 51, 54–56, 70, 71, 73, 108, 109; objectives of 51–53
monetary reform 55
money: changes 37, 45; in circulation 47–49, 68; creation 24, 32, 104; equation 41, 63; income 62, 63, 83, 100; interest rate 39, 66, 67; management of 36–56; market 12, 49, 56, 68, 83, 92, 105, 107; neutrality 64, 81; stock 32, 44; velocity 24, 103; wages 93, 101

The Nation 2
The Nation and Atheneum 2
natural interest rate 11, 12, 59, 66, 67, 72, 74, 78, 106, 109

The Nature of Capital and Income
(Fisher) 42
New Economic Policy (NEP) 22
The New Statesman 2

Ohlin, B. 35n18
Orwell, George 33

Paris Commune 17, 21
Patinkin, D. 101
Pigou, A.C. 9, 31, 101
Pigou effect 31
Pigou-Marshall-Keynes formulation 47
Pindyck, R. 35n7
planned investment 13, 61, 76
Poincare, Raymond 26, 34
Polanyi, Karl 17
political economy 9, 83
Preobrazhensky, Yevgeny 22
price deflation 30–31, 38–41, 72, 97
price equation 13, 60, 63
price flexibility 31, 52, 60
price indices 8, 12, 47, 48, 54, 58
price inflation: effects 38–41
price level 10–12, 30, 37, 42, 49, 52, 54,
56, 58, 59, 61–65, 67, 69, 73
price stability 37, 40, 67, 76
Principles of Economics (Marshall) 9
private investment 14, 19, 86, 95, 96,
102, 105, 109
profit inflation 11, 59, 66, 70
public finances 43–47, 56
public investment 14, 81, 108, 109
purchasing power: disequilibrium 69–72
*The Purchasing Power of Money: Its
Determination in Relation to Credit,
Interest and Crises* (Fisher) 41, 58, 68
purchasing power parity (PPP) 10;
theory of 50–51

quantity theory of money (QTM) 7,
10–11, 37, 47–49, 56–57, 60, 98,
105–107

Rapallo agreement 22
rapid price increase 38, 44
The Rate of Interest (Fisher) 41, 42
real balance effect 31, 97, 101–102
real interest rate 42, 73, 90
real value 19, 23, 24, 31, 38, 39, 101; of
money 38, 90, 97, 101

real wages 12, 86, 87, 93, 100, 101, 105
regulation of money: positive
suggestions 53–55
relative prices 7, 39, 74, 93, 98
Ricardo, David 10, 50
The Road to Wigan Pier (Orwell) 33
Robertson, Dennis H. 58
Robinson, Joan 75
Russian empire 17, 19

savings deposits 11, 65, 68, 69, 72
Say, Jean-Baptiste 83
Say's law 12, 83, 85–87, 98
Schumpeter, J.A. 88
Sismondi, Sismondi de 87
social unrest 21–23
Solimano, A. 35n7, 35n14
Soviet Russia 6, 20–22, 24, 25
sovznaks 25, 45
stabilisation 4, 6, 49, 51–56, 58
stock equilibrium 13
stock exchange market 19, 91, 92
stock market 1–3, 13, 34, 42, 95, 107
supply of money 23, 24, 30, 31, 36, 37,
48, 49, 53–56, 59, 69, 99

taxation 4, 9, 43–45
The Theory of Interest (Fisher) 42, 90
theory of money 47, 57, 72, 81, 93
theory of unemployment 87, 93
time and adjustment mechanisms 74–76
Togliatti, Palmiro 21
A Tract on Monetary Reform (TMR)
(Keynes) 8, 10, 12, 19, 36–56
Treatise of Versailles 20
A Treatise on Money (TM) (Keynes) 6, 8,
10–13, 57–79; analytical features of
11; Applied Theory of Money 72–73;
banking system 65–66; bank rate
66–67; fundamental equations of 62–
64; monetary-financial mechanism
77–79; Pure Theory of Money 61–62;
reactions and comments 74
The Treatise on Probability (Keynes) 5

uncertainty 5
under-consumption 87
unemployment 4, 8, 9, 13, 14, 30–32, 34,
70, 80, 93, 100, 101, 104
United States 17, 18, 20; depression to
recovery 31–33

value of money 57, 61; dynamics of
  changes 68–69
value theory 7, 93
Versailles Conference of 1919 1
Viner, J. 97n9
voluntary unemployment 86

wage rigidity 76, 97, 99–101
Walras, Leon 74, 83
Walras law 58, 83
war reparations 6, 19, 24, 27–30, 34

Weimar Republic 20
Wicksell, Knut 11, 58, 67, 106
Wicksellian mechanism 105
world economy 2, 16, 30, 57
World War I 19; broader
  consequences of 20–21
World War I (WWI) 17–19

Young, Owen D. 27
Young Plan of 1929/1930 27,
  28, 34

For Product Safety Concerns and Information please contact our EU
representative GPSR@taylorandfrancis.com
Taylor & Francis Verlag GmbH, Kaufingerstraße 24, 80331 München, Germany